The Vast
and the
Spurious

25 Problems For Feminism

The Vast and the Spurious

Duncan Smith

Alfadex Books

Published by Alfadex Books, Sydney, 2019.
Copyright © Duncan Smith 2019.

A CIP catalogue record for this book is available from the National Library of Australia.
ISBN 978-0-9872228-4-8

1. Gender Studies 2. Feminism 3. Social Criticism.

Alfadex Books orders and information
Email: matthew.alfadex@gmail.com

Duncan Smith is guitarist and songwriter with the band Lighthouse XIII, whose albums include *Waves Upon Waves*, *Vortex Winder*, *The Maelstrom Ascendant*, and *Cultown*.

He is the author of the books *The Vortex Winder*, *The Maelstrom Ascendant*, *Cultown*, and *The Tightarse Tuesday Book Club*.

Website – www.vortexwinder.com

Contents

1

Twenty-Five Problems

This book discusses twenty-five problems with feminism. One of the main problems is you're not allowed to criticise it in the first place. As I'm going to do so at some length, this will make me a target for attack. In that case, I'll start by explaining my position and why this book has been written.

Some people think any critic of feminism must be a right wing thug who wants to send women back to the 1950s. But I believe women should have the same rights as men and be free to pursue any goal. Why shouldn't they? Still, supporting the fair reforms of the 1970s doesn't mean you have to endorse the cultish fanaticism that goes on today.

Of course, a movement as big as feminism doesn't exist without reason. On some topics feminists are right, on others they are wrong. The aim of this book, *The Vast and the Spurious*, is to try to understand which ones. Where they are right, their efforts may lead to a better world. But where they are wrong, their mistakes will lead to a worse world - for everyone. #Feminism hurts women too.

I am male. For some, that disqualifies me from having an opinion on this subject. But as the modern agenda consists of hectoring men about their enormous power and privilege, it's clear feminism is not just about women's issues. They will accuse me of 'man-splaining' feminism, but as feminists have been woman-splaining for years how patriarchy ruined their lives, it's only fair to return fire. Still, in deference to those who've gone before, let's start with the ceremonial rites.

Acknowledging the Traditional Owners of The Land

As a man writing on this topic, I'd like to acknowledge the Traditional Owners of Gender Studies: feminists.

Apparently they own the land. They get very angry if a man trespasses on that land by having a voice, or even a thought, about gender issues. This anger may be cloaked in the pretence that they don't care what men think. They will sometimes declare, with passionate indifference, just how much they don't care. Indeed, when it comes to feminist books, it seems to be a genre convention for authors to assert that they 'don't give a fuck' what men think of their field. Clementine Ford says this in chapter eight of her book. Jessa Crispin says it in chapter seven of hers. Probably a hundred other women have said it in theirs.

This is really a wonderful liberation for a fellow like me, for when I began writing this book, an inner voice would often be nagging away about whether feminists would approve. It's a great relief to learn that they don't care what any man thinks.

Still, having entered the field of feminist writing, it's only polite to observe the genre conventions with the ritual words: I don't give a fuck what men think about feminism. There. Was that OK?

Now the formalities are over, let's get on with the book.

A Few Points to Begin

To be honest, that was a lie. I do care what people think, and maybe this book can even change a few minds. Not the hardcore feminists, of course. That will never happen. But the book isn't written for them. It is for the open-minded woman or man who wants to hear a different view than the media allows. It's for the kid starting university about to be force-fed identity politics for the next three years. It's for those sick of the one-sidedness of the conversation.

Still, before criticising feminism in detail, it's worth remembering why it exists, and the sort of thing that fired women up in the seventies and sometimes still goes on today. For example, I recall one time from my own university days when a pompous male academic lectured for an hour, then also dominated the tute group that followed. We sure got sick of his voice. Then there was a recent YouTube clip where a young woman gave a brilliant performance on the bass guitar. One of the top comments was 'the best part of this video is her smile.' This retro chauvinism would easily make that *Everyday Sexism* website.

So, while this is mainly an anti-feminist book, it is sympathetic to them when they have a fair point. Apart from being a matter of ethical fair play, there's more chance of changing people's minds if you show some empathy rather than just trying to blast them into oblivion. They might then start to listen and empathise with you too. Of course, if that doesn't work, you can always fall back on plan B, which is to blast them into oblivion.

In the same spirit, this book won't be taking any cheap shots at the physical appearance of any feminists. That sort of personal attack is irrelevant, and reflects badly on the attacker. Behavioural ugliness on the other hand - such as lying, bullying, or slandering - will be called out whoever is doing it.

For the record, I support some of the basic feminist causes, such as equal pay for the same work and a fair deal on housework and parenting. Ironically, the only way feminists will ever actually solve those problems is to stop lying about the 'gender pay gap.' That is, lying about its real nature and causes.

As for whether males and females have the same innate abilities, let's just say people should be treated as individuals, and get the benefit of the doubt until proven otherwise.

As for other issues, I support women's right to sexual freedom and to not have to face blatant sexual harassment, but oppose the recent excesses of the Me Too movement.

Then there's rape and domestic violence. It's pretty obvious stuff, you would think. Domestic violence, for instance. You mean it's *wrong* to beat up your own family? Who knew? But that applies whichever gender is doing it. Contrary to popular belief, it doesn't just go one way.

What I chiefly oppose in feminism are some key delusions, some behavioural traits, and the overall mental climate these create. Among the main delusions are that women are always worse off than men, and that men are always villains and women victims. Another problem is the fixation on gender where it has no relevance.

As for behaviour, I oppose the feminist attempt to leverage historical suffering for present day gain, and its culture of bullying and intimidation. The overall climate all this creates is one of hatred between the sexes. While this is not all the fault of feminists, they have certainly played their part.

Origins of this Book

This book was prompted by several events, of which two stand out. One was reading a newspaper article about 'male privilege,' which is the idea that men are better off than women in almost all areas of life. The implication was that men cruise through life as pampered lords, while women struggle through like the damned in Hades.

The other event happened when the book was already half written. It was the attempted screening in Australia of a film called *The Red Pill*, which gave a sympathetic hearing to men's rights activists (MRAs). This was an act of profanity for feminists, who protested and got the film banned. MRAs are those who challenge the feminist premise that women are always the disadvantaged sex. What's striking about *The Red*

Pill is it started out as a hit piece on MRAs, but its female filmmaker changed her mind once she got to know them. This was pure heresy for feminists, who called it a propaganda film. That was odd, because when I finally got to see the film, it turned out to be an *alternative* to the feminist propaganda we normally get in the media.

Really, *The Red Pill* just offered another view on gender issues, but the whole protest debacle shows there is something deeply wrong with feminism today. If the way you deal with critics is to silence them or lie about them, this is highly revealing about the sort of movement you are.

So, *The Red Pill* is 'a propaganda film,' is it? If by propaganda they mean *someone's opinion*, then we are all propagandists. The difference is some people get to deliver their propaganda through national, mainstream media. Clementine Ford, for example, writes one or two newspaper columns a week - and while Ford is a formidable warrior for her cause, she only ever argues one side. Still, by all means read her columns and books. Then for the sake of balance, go and listen to a YouTube talk by Janice Fiamengo or Karen Straughan.

Karen Straughan is one of those evil men's rights activists you hear about. She's popular with men due to her eccentric penchant for not hating their guts. I had actually never heard of MRAs when I began writing this book. Since then, and after watching *The Red Pill*, I've heard a good deal more about them.

Feminists need to move on from the idea that they have a monopoly on sorrow. Injustice takes various forms and is experienced by many types of people - even some of those white males they think are so privileged.

This book was originally two long essays. The first was called 'Agony: Much Worse Than Yours,' (meant humorously, of course). It looked at twelve problems to do with the idea of male privilege. The second essay, 'The Vast and the Spurious,' looked at a further twelve problems.

I've kept those original 'problems' and spread them out over the chapters of the book. Some are dealt with briefly, others at much greater length. Problem 25 will make up the last chapter.

Some of these are problems *with* feminism in terms of its beliefs, or how it is done. A few are problems *for* feminism, in the sense of being legitimate issues that women face. For example, problems 12-14 are sympathetic to them. Here is a full list, with the names I've given them.

1. Trump or the Tramp
2. The CEO Problem: Check Explanation, OK
3. It's Not 1970 Anymore
4. Female Privilege
5. Agony: Much Worse Than Yours

6. We Are Not a Gestalt
7. Gender Doesn't Matter
8. How Dare You Resist My Attack?
9. Big Sister is Watching You
10. Misogyny vs. Misandry

11. The Gender Pay Gap
12. Yes, That's Annoying
13. The Weight of History
14. Dickheads Anonymous
15. It's Still Not 1970

16. What Ya Gonna Do?
17. Bullshit or Not?
18. Whinge, Whine, WTF
19. So Fucking What?
20. Stop Caring What People Think

21. Assert Yourself or Die
22. Do Something
23. Give Me My Privilege!
24. Turning Male Problems into Male Privilege
25. Addicted to Feminism

Apart from these twenty-five problems, the book has five main parts. Chapters 2-4 are about male privilege. Chapters 5-8 discuss the capacity for evil in both men and women, and respond to a feminist's attack on MRAs. Chapters 9-12 deal with the gender pay gap, and the battle over work in and outside the home. Chapters 13-17 return to male privilege. Then, chapters 18 and 19 complete the book, and include the Utopian vision, 'A Dream of Fecunda.'

It's worth noting that this book is about Western nations, and does not discuss feminism or the position of women outside the West.

Footnote on the Essay Titles

Agony: Much Worse Than Yours refers to the song, 'Agony,' from the Sondheim musical, *Into the Woods*. The Vast and the Spurious is of course a play on *The Fast and the Furious* film series.

2

Agony:
Much Worse Than Yours

The Basic Premise - Male Privilege

The basic premise of feminism today is the idea of 'male privilege' - meaning a series of advantages for men and injustices for women. The idea is that women are deeply disadvantaged compared to men. There is profound bias against them and obstacles placed in their way. A key point is that the privilege is *unearned*. It's a series of benefits men enjoy simply by being men.

Male privilege falls into two broad categories, as I see it. The first is to do with opportunities, wealth, and power; the second with social norms and behaviour.

A recent public debate asked 'is male privilege bullshit?' Some feminists remarked that male privilege is such a certain and established fact it's not even open to debate. Yet presumably some people *do* think it's bullshit. Well, whether the theory of male privilege is a truth, an exaggeration, or an illusion, it surely needs more discussion before we accept it as a scientific fact.

One problem with the idea of male-privilege-as-fact is that the group who hates it the most - feminists - also owe their existence to it. What happens if male privilege comes to an end? Does that also mean the end of feminism?

It's an odd dynamic. A group has a strong opposition to something but also a vested interest in believing in it, as it is their *raison d'être* and the motor that drives them forward. Though they may hate it, feminists have stronger motivation to believe in male privilege than to disbelieve it. This can lead to a questionable relationship with the evidence.

It may turn out the theory of male privilege is true. If so, feminists will have been proven right. But there are a lot of objections to overcome before that day arrives. This book will raise twenty-five problems for the theory of male privilege, or for feminism itself.

Some of these are discussed only briefly - there are five in this chapter - while others will get one or more chapters to themselves.

Problem 1 - Trump and the Tramp

Feminists seem convinced men have much more power than women and are advantaged in every aspect of life. But this requires a selective view of the evidence.

Let's look at one of feminism's most hated figures - US President Donald Trump. Those who believe in male privilege look at Trump, a powerful white male, but they don't look at the tramp in the street. A comment on a news article about male privilege was, 'Did you trip on the 80% male homeless on your way to the office to write this?'

Almost everyone falls prey to this sort of bias, to sifting the evidence in favour of their own cause or theory. If you believe women are the only ones victimised, it's easy to find data to support this while ignoring other data which disagrees. If you think men have more power, you see Trump but not the tramp. You look at all the male CEOs, but not the guys in the dole queue or working minimum wage.

Many ordinary men listen bemused to the tales of their enormous power. They start looking for their male privilege card to see if the warranty's still valid. Maybe they can send it back for a refund.

A recent YouTube video about privilege implied being born

a white male automatically gets you a 'level 6 management position,' whatever that is. Although this idea is based on statistics, they're still generalising about an entire group.

Statistics can be misleading. Imagine there are ten guys in a room and one of them has a million bucks and the other nine have nothing. On average, each of them has $100, 000.

If there's a woman in the next room with $80, 000 and you tell her the guys next door have 100K each, she starts to resent all of them, not just the millionaire. That's the trouble with a term like male privilege. It joins a lot of individuals into a group entity, then encourages anyone outside that group to think they're all the same.

Of course, I chose those statistics - a millionaire and nine tramps - because it suited my argument. Easy, isn't it?

The theory of male privilege is an attempt to fight sexism, but to some degree 'male privilege' is a sexist term in itself. It's a pejorative that invites people to make negative assumptions about people based purely on their gender. In the same way, 'white male privilege' is sexist and racist, promoting a mindset of *justified resentment* against individuals based on their sex and race.

That's one tyranny of the age of identity politics - putting people into groups and making stupid assumptions about them because they belong to that group. It's worth memorising the following slogan:

We discriminate when we fail to discriminate.

We treat people unjustly when we don't see them as individuals. To 'discriminate' is not always a bad thing. If you say, 'Captain Bligh punished the crew indiscriminately,' it means he mistreated them all the same. When we discriminate among different things, we see them *as* different and judge them on their individual merit, not as part of a herd.

10

While it is easy to generalise about certain demographics, the risk is encouraging hostility towards the group as a whole, rather than those individuals who may actually deserve it. We discriminate when we fail to discriminate

Throwing the term 'white male privilege' around as a term of abuse isn't a good strategy because it causes one group to resent another, and the target group to resent the first because of their resentment. In reality, most of us aren't Donald Trump. We're a lot closer to the tramp.

Note: My problem 1 is also known as the 'apex fallacy.'

Problem 2 - The CEO Problem: Check Explanation,OK

There are many more male than female CEOs. This is often cited as proof of bias against women. This sort of reasoning is superficial, for it doesn't examine the causes of this fact, or question if becoming a CEO is even worthwhile in the first place.

There are lots of reasons people do or don't go down the path of managing large corporations. In my own case, one among *many* reasons I'm not a CEO is I have no desire to work sixty hour weeks or take on the burden of running a company. I'd rather spend time with my wife and on creative work, even if it pays less. I also chose to study the arts and humanities at university, rather than finance or business - a choice which greatly reduced my chances of becoming a CEO. Not that I ever had the ability in the first place.

Many women have made similar choices in their education - but even the ones in business may not want to be CEOs. An ex-girlfriend of mine worked for a global corporation and rose to a fairly high level, but had no wish to go higher as she didn't want to lose her leisure time and private life.

Although her salary was several times my own, I never

thought of her as having 'privilege.' She just worked in a very different job as a result of her career choices.

It's easy to point to low numbers of female CEOs and say, 'there you go, clear proof of male privilege,' but this is to reduce complex causality down to a simple focus on gender. If you really want to understand who becomes CEOs, you have to look at all the causal factors that go into it, one of which is motivation. As well as asking 'how do you become a CEO?' another question is 'why would you want to?' In some respects, CEOs are to be pitied rather than envied. Most of them are probably workaholics with heavy responsibilities, little time for their partners, and even less for their children.

I've only ever personally known one CEO. Let's call him Steve. He came to me for lessons many years ago when I was teaching music. Steve never had time to practice. He showed up once a week for his lesson, then had no chance to practice before the next one. Too busy being a CEO! Were the lessons a waste of money? Maybe, but he had plenty of that - he was a multi-millionaire. What he didn't have was time. In that sense, he was a pauper.

Steve loved his children but didn't have much time to see them. Then, a couple of years before his fiftieth birthday, the poor guy collapsed and died, even though he seemed in good health. He left behind a wife and three young kids. It makes you wonder: if Steve had his time over, would he choose to go down that whole CEO path in the first place?

When it comes to CEOs and privilege, though, there's another side to the story. Professor Jonty J. Jones of Equity University recently did a groundbreaking new study of the 'CEO Problem' but instead focused on the *partners* of male CEOs. In a shock finding, it turned out most of them were attractive, heterosexual females. Some of these people, despite limited education, business training, or work ethic were able to use their Beauty Privilege and Reproductive Privilege to enjoy lives of affluence on the same level as their CEO husbands. Hypergamy: you've gotta love it.

This is a shocking example of gender privilege in the world of CEOs. If the vast majority of CEOs choose pretty heterosexual females as their partners, this clearly discriminates against gay men, lesbians, and less attractive women. What should we do about this? Perhaps if male CEOs *insist* on choosing attractive women as wives, they should be legally compelled to also support a mistress from one of the disadvantaged groups.

As you can see, the 'CEO problem' is a many splendored thing. Is it a knock-down argument that proves the existence of male privilege? Er ... maybe not.

The CEO problem? Check Explanation, OK.

Problem 3 - It's Not 1970 Anymore

A recent cartoon on Facebook showed a footrace in which the man's running lane was empty but the woman's lane was full of traps, obstacles, and impediments. To which you might say, '1970 called and wants its cartoon back.'

Everyone knows women's opportunities were limited before then. They faced many restrictions on what they could do, and obstacles to their progress. 1970s second-wave feminism was entitled to protest this.

Yet some feminists seem to think we're still living in 1970. They speak as if women still have no power, and face traps and obstacles at every step of the way like nothing has changed in fifty years.

In many professional fields it is no longer the case, at least in the West - and to be clear, my book is only about women in Western democracies. The position of women outside the West is very different but that's another story. In our society, barring unusual circumstances, girls can now pursue careers in science, engineering, law, business, and scores of other professions far more easily than they could fifty years ago.

Even so, some feminist books still claim girls are socialised into so called 'feminine' professions and away from 'masculine' ones. Apparently some girls don't know they're allowed to go into business now, and can even go down the path of becoming a CEO if they want. Then again, you'd have to say girls who don't know that probably aren't CEO material in the first place.

Almost any intelligent girl in the West must realise by now she can choose the subjects she studies and the career she pursues. This was not so in the past. For example, in the obscure 1977 book, *What Society Does to Girls*, Joyce Nicholson bitterly recalls the limited career and education choices available to girls of her generation. But that was decades ago. There are now many initiatives which encourage girls to pursue whatever careers they want to. In Western nations, unless you're talking about the Amish or other retro communities, most girls know they have career options.

Some people think there's a force called 'Social Expectations' which stops girls knowing that, and brainwashes them into choosing certain jobs over others. One would hope that in 2019, most girls realise they can study engineering, law, etc, rather than whatever retro profession Social Expectations are forcing them to enter.

It's true that in many professions people feel that they have little power, and face traps and obstacles at every step of the way - and many of those people are men. Most professions are hierarchical and hard to advance in - for both genders. The idea that being male guarantees an easy ride to the top is an illusion.

If there are professions where women *are* discriminated against, you can only address each one in turn. With regard to something like sexual harassment, which does affect women more than men, what can anyone say except the obvious? Sexual harassment should play no part in professional life.

There are still some professions where women face obstacles, but overall it's clear a lot has changed in fifty years. To listen to some feminists, you might not know it. They still seem to think girls have no control over their educational and career choices, and are little more than corks bobbing around on the stormy seas of the patriarchy.

The world is certainly not perfect in 2019, but it's not 1970 anymore. Stop pretending it is.

Problem 4 - Check Your Female Privilege

There are advantages and disadvantages for both sexes. This was even true in 1970. For example, your chances of being drafted to the Vietnam war were somewhat higher if you were male.

Now, fifty years later, there are still benefits and drawbacks for either sex. Yet feminists would have us believe men have the better deal in every part of life. This is why men are urged to the self castigation of 'checking' their privilege. You're supposed to berate yourself for your unearned good fortune. Don't overlook that word, by the way. *Unearned*. It's an important concept.

As mentioned, one might divide privilege into two broad categories. The first is around basic issues of health, work, and power, while the second is in social norms and behaviour. It's true women have come off worse in some areas, but hardly all of them. Here is a quick glance at the topic, with a few examples.

If you're male, you're statistically more likely to have a high paid job and work in politics, media, or senior management. You may face less scrutiny over clothes, and your behaviour (although in the age of Me Too, this has changed). If you become a parent, you won't have to take time off from your career to give birth. You're less likely to be sexually harassed.

You might also see more men in film and TV roles.

On the downside, you're statistically more likely to die younger, work longer, abuse drugs and alcohol, or commit suicide. Your gender presently does worse in school and university. You're more likely to be a victim of violence, and will get tougher sentencing than a woman if you commit the same crime. If your marriage fails, you may face discrimination over child custody. As these privilege lists are always seen in terms of one group versus another, female privilege can be inferred by reversing all the items in this paragraph. More examples of female privilege will be given later in the book.

These are a few broad strokes. There are plenty of online sources that discuss male privilege in detail, and a lot less that address female privilege. One should approach all such information with some caution, as there's not much neutrality around this topic.

For now, the idea that everything is stacked in favour of men is pretty hard to believe. The claim that there are no benefits to being female and no downsides to being male just doesn't fly.

Surely feminists' case would be more plausible if they said, 'There are *some* benefits to being female and drawbacks to being male, but overall you've still got the better deal.' To be fair, some do say that, although not very often. You'll also sometimes hear the line *patriarchy hurts men too*, and the unspoken rest of the sentence will always be *but nowhere near as much*.

And that brings us to the next problem.

Problem 5 - Agony: Much Worse Than Yours

Overall, you don't hear much from feminists about female privilege. The whole narrative is about how hard life is for women compared to men.

Again, many a man feels bemused by the rumours of his

amazing power and how easy life is. If he asked a hardcore feminist, 'do you think you're the only ones who suffer prejudice and injustice?' she might reply, *Of course not. So do people of colour, gays, transgenders, Muslims,* (and the rest of the usual victim groups). If the man, who is also white, says 'I too have suffered,' the feminist may well laugh in his face. The laughter means, *How can you suffer? You've got white male privilege.*

The man might make his case and even if he could prove he'd suffered a little, the next response would be something about 'male tears.' *Cry me a river, white boy. Your suffering's a drop in the ocean compared to ours.*

In other words, you could never persuade a hardcore feminist of the Buddhist view that all creatures suffer! It's always a case of women's pain being worse. The perfect theme song for this would be 'Agony' from Sondheim's musical, *Into the Woods.* There's a scene where two lovelorn princes are trying to woo princesses, and competing to see who is suffering the most heartbreak. One of them sings, *Agony: much more terrible than yours!* Or something along those lines.

That is more or less the default feminist response to any claims of male suffering. You see, to quote a different song title, they have a 'monopoly on sorrow.' When it comes time to sup from the great pool of sorrow, there isn't much left once women and all the other oppressed groups have had their turn. White males are the only group immune to life's vale of tears.

Apart from being highly simplistic, this idea is of course racist and sexist in itself. But that doesn't bother those for whom racism and sexism seem to matter so much.

The song 'Monopoly on Sorrow' is by a band called Suicidal Tendencies. That's fitting, because the suicide rate is far higher in men than in women. But you must never mention anything to do with male problems. As a leading men's rights activist said, any talk about male suffering doesn't draw sympathy, but *anger*! That's because no matter what happens, the suffering of women will always be Agony: so painful, much worse than yours.

A well known feminist is fond of dismissing men's rights activists as 'whiny man babies.' This is not a good strategy. First, it invites the observation that, in those terms, the entire edifice of feminism is based upon 'whining.' Second, it's unwise to treat your fellow human beings with such belittling contempt. It's hard to see why they should have any sympathy for you if you have none for them.

We've now come to the end of the chapter, so let's finish with one more refrain of that plaintive yet rollicking chorus. All together now: Agony: so painful, much worse than yours!

3

We Are Not a Gestalt

Problem 6 - We Are Not a Gestalt

Some Christians believe that because of original sin by Adam and Eve, all human beings live in a permanent state of guilt and have to repent.

Some feminists believe that because of historical crimes of men against women, all today's men live in a permanent state of guilt and have to repent. Not only that, they have to pay reparations - for the sins they never committed.

It may be true that in past eras social systems favoured men, and there were many specific crimes by men against women. But despite what people may think, there is no connection whatever between men alive today and those alive in past eras. In the same way, there is no connection at all between women alive today and those in the past.

We are not a gestalt.

Some people want to join a lot of different individuals, dispersed in time and space, into a vast amorphous collective and treat it like a single entity. Any member of that group is then supposed to feel guilt for sins committed by other members, and make reparations.

The idea that women were historically maligned and should now have equal opportunity is fair. The idea that they should get preferential treatment is not. To some degree, 'reverse discrimination' is opportunism masquerading as justice. It's an attempt to leverage historical suffering for present day gain. In other words, some women today seek reparations for suffering they did not experience, and to punish men for crimes *they* did not commit.

Again, there is not some gestalt entity known as 'men' any more than there's a gestalt entity known as 'women.'

We should certainly learn from the past and not repeat its mistakes. But some want to impose a guilt narrative onto the entire male gender, who must make amends by giving females preferential treatment in everything. These are the reparations today's men are supposed to make - for the crimes they never committed.

It sounds a bit like a quest for ... what's that phrase again? Ah yes - *unearned privilege*.

Today's women should have the same rights and opportunities as men. They should be given jobs if they have the best credentials - but not just due to the historical suffering of other people to whom they have no connection except having the same type of genitals.

Problem 7 - Gender Doesn't Matter

Having said that, there are some areas where reform is justified. In industries that have been male-dominated for no good reason, it's fair to take steps to encourage women to enter them. However, once that short term goal is achieved, the real aim is a meritocracy.

A meritocracy is a system where jobs and rewards are given based on ability, rather than irrelevant factors like race, sex, money, connections, and so on. A meritocracy is so remote from our present world it seems Utopian, but it's always worth trying. Still, you don't achieve it by substituting a new form of discrimination for the old one.

An exception might be dealing with disabled people, who should be helped - but women aren't disabled. That's the point, isn't it? That women are every bit as capable as men.

That's why it was laughable to see a recent news story about

Cambridge University trying to ban the use of words like 'genius' and 'brilliant' as they contain 'assumptions of gender inequality' and might intimidate female students.

If you didn't know better, you'd think this came from a satirical newspaper like *The Onion*. Who comes up with this stuff? A female academic, as it turned out. It's condescending nonsense that treats women like slow-witted children who have to be helped.

The story got a strong response from women in the comments sections, e.g. 'I'm a woman and I'm brilliant. Stop treating us like we're idiots.' And, 'May I politely suggest that Dr X kindly buggers off somewhere else to teach this crappola, and also if there are any women that are somehow threatened by these words, they REALLY should not be at Cambridge because there is absolutely NO HOPE for them! What a walking disgrace (and I'm a woman!)'

In a meritocracy, reward is based only on ability and achievement. Yet it's true no one can show their ability unless given a chance. I'm well aware of the 'Matthew Effect,' which is the principle that those who are already 'rich,' so to speak, will be given more, and those who are poor will lose even what they have. But the Matthew Effect applies to lots of demographics, and for many different reasons. It doesn't just align with gender in some simplistic way.

We should try to help disadvantaged groups, for example, victims of poverty cycles. If meritocracy is the goal, we must give people a chance to compete. You start by giving equal access to education, and encouraging people to use their abilities. From there, it's anyone's game.

There is a profound confusion between equality of opportunity and equality of outcome. Some people think gender equality is only achieved in a given industry when there is a fifty-fifty split between men and women. This is to take gender obsession to the point of absurdity. What's more, the focus on equality of outcome is likely to cause far more injustice than it prevents.

Equality is achieved when men and women have the same opportunity to train for a profession and can get a job in it based on their individual merits. If there are unfair obstacles, these should be addressed. But each industry is different so you need to look at each one in turn, rather than mindlessly enforcing a fifty-fifty male-female quota. For one thing, gender should be irrelevant to most professions. For another, there are many forms of discrimination besides gender.

If men and women have equal ability, as feminists contend, then as long as everyone has equal access to education, jobs can be given out purely on merit. Then let's say there is an industry with a higher number of men and a feminist complains, the response should be two words: *so what?*

Little is achieved by giving out jobs based on gender quotas, even as an attempt to right historical wrongs. Let's say there was a case where a female was a better applicant but missed the job. She could rightly complain about discrimination. But if a male applicant was better and missed out, he could complain too. He might then hear something about 'male tears' with the implication that 'we were discriminated against for centuries, so suck it up, it's your turn.' To which he might reply, '*You* weren't discriminated against. A lot of other women were, but not *you*.'

Enforcing 50% gender quotas is silly for two main reasons. First, it goes against the ideal of meritocracy. Let's say there are ten jobs up for grabs and out of the ten best applicants, eight are women and two are men. In that case, the jobs should go to eight women and two men, not five women and five men. But the other main reason quotas are silly is it's an attempt to force the tedious issue of gender on fields which have nothing to do with gender.

Take the Triple J Hottest 100 songs for popular music in Australia. The low number of female artists in the top 100 has been cited as yet another case of male privilege. So, presumably, some people want to ensure fifty of the top hundred songs each year are by female artists.

As soon as you start imposing quotas here, you're fixating on something irrelevant. Popular music is about arranging musical notes, words, and beats in various ways. Anyone can arrange those basic elements as they please. Anyone can learn a musical instrument. Possession of a penis or a vagina has nothing to do with the ability to play or write music.

It's not as if there are no role models in popular music. Janis Joplin and Suzi Quatro had their careers a *long* time ago. Angela Gossow and Alissa White-Gluz have both fronted the heavy metal band, Arch Enemy. Taylor Swift and Beyonce are two of the biggest pop stars.

The chances of girls making a career in pop music these days are the same as anyone else's - shitty! Showbiz has always been tough to get into and, in some ways, the music business today is as bad as it's ever been. But that's the same for both genders.

There's a long litany of sins of which the music biz, and showbiz in general, is guilty. A truly 'diverse' series of injustices. Prejudice against those who are too old, who don't look right, or play unfashionable genres; those who don't like touring, are introverts, or lack business skills and legal knowledge. The list goes on.

Still, if we're concerned about the Top 100 representing different groups, why stop at gender? What about the awful conspiracy against left-handed people? The striking shortage of Buddhist rappers? The obvious dearth of transgender trombonists.

Most pertinent of all, how about the appalling treatment of bald people before 1990? Does anyone know that before baldness became socially acceptable, there were only two hairless Australian rock stars? That's Peter Garrett and Angry Anderson. Australia's shameful era of Hair Privilege is something all kids should learn about in schools. Indeed today's bald rock musicians should all get record deals to make up for the hair prejudice suffered by those in the 1960s-80s to whom they have no connection.

How about other special interest groups - LGBT, disabled, single parents, geriatrics, vegetarians, refugees? The Hottest 100 will never show true diversity until all these groups are represented. Of course, none of those categories have anything to do with music.

Having said that quotas are silly, it's worth repeating they sometimes do have 'merit,' so to speak. In formerly male-dominated fields, it may be worthwhile to include some women to broaden people's ideas of what is normal and possible. It's good to see some female scientists on TV, or discussing politics, sport, or whatever male-dominated area may once have been. But as to whether we're dealing with a vast problem or a spurious problem, you'd have to look at each industry in turn.

Finally, it's always good to see Judge Judy on TV, starring as one of the most well known representatives of the legal profession. Important to note, though, Judge Judy got there on merit. She didn't make it because she was a woman. She made it because she was brilliant.

4

Big Sister is Watching You

Problem 8 - How Dare You Resist My Attack?

Imagine someone starts an argument and insults you. You defend yourself and are instantly accused of harassment.

How about a female comedian who holds up a wax model of a severed bloody head, meant to be that of a male politician? When the stunt draws a backlash, she seems surprised.

Let's not forget that time a meeting of men's rights activists was shut down by feminist protesters. When the protest leader began reading a prepared statement, an MRA interrupted her and was told to 'Shut the fuck up - I'm reading!'

What about a feminist's likely reaction to my own book, which might be: *Who are you to write a book on feminism? What could you know about women's experience?* To which I might reply: isn't your whole career about attacking men and toxic masculinity?

Or, as Karen Straughan said, what would we think of a movement that attacks an entire gender by equating patriarchy with evil and feminism with good? If you're a man, you'd better not question the idea - just shut up and listen.

Milo Yiannopoulos once spoke of a feminist who tweeted about 'pathetic and threatened men,' then tried to pretend there was something shocking about receiving strong criticism. 'This is the essence of the cry-bully,' he said. 'The person who dishes it out but cannot take it...and everybody knows this from arguments with the women in their lives...who come in all guns blazing, hurling insults and physical objects, and then the slightest attempt at restraint or response and suddenly the man is the bad guy... an abusive monster.'

These are all examples of 'How dare you resist my attack?' - a state of mind which assumes the right to attack others without reprisal. It's also a license to behave towards your opponents in ways you would never accept from them. But these are the times we're living in - as the next section will show.

Problem 9 - Big Sister is Watching You

It is a sad truth that some movements which start in liberation end in oppression. Revolutions turn into regimes. How do you know your movement has become a regime? Theories become facts, criticism is not allowed, and the critics themselves are silenced or slandered.

Feminism was a liberation movement in the 1970s when it fought for women to have the same freedom as men. Many of its reforms were justified. Yet fifty years later we're told women are still deeply disadvantaged. 'Male privilege' is a series of profound biases against women. Today's men must accept this as fact and make reparations for the crimes of the past.

Feminists are entitled to make this case - but others should be allowed to question it. So, are they?

A 2017 public debate in Australia had the topic 'Is Male Privilege Bullshit?' This annoyed two local feminists, Ruby Hamad and Clementine Ford, who said male privilege is now an established fact and no longer up for debate. As proof, Hamad cited the gender pay gap, domestic violence, the number of women in media and politics, the lack of female CEOs, and the Triple J Hottest 100 pop songs.

Those arguments are flawed anyway, but more disturbing is the attempt to shut down the debate. We're asked to accept male privilege as if it's a scientific fact - but scientists are supposed to put their theories up for critique. They're meant to be neutral observers seeking the truth, and must allow their theories to be questioned. In practice, many scientists love their theories and treat them with protective bias.

I've read many of Clementine Ford's articles and her two books. While she's a serious activist for her cause could she, in any seriousness, claim to be a neutral participant in her field? Yet we're supposed to accept her verdict that male privilege is a fact and she's just relaying the bad news.

In her opinion piece on male privilege, Ruby Hamad also took aim at men's rights activists (MRAs). She said their movement lacks the intellectual and ethical rigor of feminism. She went on to dismiss MRAs' motivation as a wish to bring back the 'good old days' of male dominance. As later chapters will explain, that claim is false - and there's no intellectual or ethical rigor in such a trite dismissal of your critics.

Ruby's main work is in the field of race and she has since gone on to her own battles with white feminists. Her most famous article is called 'How white women use strategic tears to silence women of colour' - but that's another story.

Strangely, some of those crying women also make sarcastic reference to 'male tears' when it suits them. These are the male tears which feminists apparently want to drink out of tea cups. But we mustn't forget that those tears are barely enough to *fill* one of those cups, compared to the female tears which come down in such plenty as to fill Niagara Falls. Lest we forget whose agony will always be much worse than yours.

Sarcastic jibes about male tears are a way of trying to shame men into silence. Another tactic is the word 'mansplaining,' which originally meant a man explaining something to a woman in a condescending way. It now extends to disapproval of men having an opinion at all. *Oh there goes so and so, having an opinion again. Just more of his damn mansplaining.* Apparently, the right thing for men to do when feminists speak is shut up and listen.

Ruby Hamad doesn't want people debating the idea of male privilege. They must accept it as fact. And part of your 'privilege' is you don't get to defend your own gender if you disagree with Hamad's views. As someone commented on her article, 'Since identity politics insists on dividing people up into teams, here's how it is...she wants to be allowed to barrack for her team, but the opposition is not allowed to barrack for *their* team.'

It's worth noting a couple of sarcastic tweets that came out after the debate on male privilege. One person said they were looking forward to a debate about whether the Holocaust happened. Another said the next debate should be about whether slavery is good or bad.

The first tweet implies male privilege is as factual as the Holocaust. This is an odd comparison. The Holocaust is a specific event that happened over a few years. Male privilege is a complicated theory that interprets the whole of social history up to the present day, covering thousands of years and hundreds of societies. The tweet is comparing a factual event with a complicated theory. Jewish people don't think of the Holocaust as a theory.

Also revealing is the choice of comparison. Apparently the position of Western women compares to the Holocaust and slavery. That's the sort of analogy that occurs to them. If this is the level of delusion, there had better be more debates as soon as possible. If this is what male privilege theorists actually believe, we are in deep trouble and should view their other statements with caution.

We can also note the moral subtext of the tweets. Anyone who denies male privilege is like a Holocaust-denier. Anyone who questions it is akin to a slave owner.

If the second tweeter was talking about the status of women through history, you *could* make a comparison with slavery, but even that's a stretch. Yet the debate topic 'is male privilege bullshit?' was about the present day, not the past.

Still, Twitter is a notoriously casual medium for thought, and words can be banged out pretty quickly. Perhaps whoever tweeted those comments would withdraw them on greater reflection. At least, you would hope so.

The Red Pill

The most telling sign we're living under the 'Big Sister Is Watching You' regime was the fuss over the film *The Red Pill* in 2017. This documentary was made by a feminist named Cassie Jaye, who began researching MRAs. The film didn't work out as planned. Talking to MRAs led Jaye to question her own worldview, before finally reaching a more balanced view of gender relations.

It's a novel concept, isn't it? Listening to your critics, allowing counter arguments, and even changing your views as a result. This is the model for how an academic or scientist is *supposed* to behave.

The Red Pill is heresy as it questions the core feminist belief that women are far worse off than men. It also humanises, rather than demonises, men's rights activists. One film critic even slammed it for doing exactly that. At any rate, the film raises some interesting questions. Any feminist with an interest in truth rather than just power, should at least consider it a useful counter-opinion.

So what did Australian feminists do about *The Red Pill?* Sit down and watch it with an open mind then follow up with some reflection and a civil discussion? No, that would be the behaviour of a Utopian world very distant from our own.

What really happened was a series of aggressive protests to stop the film being screened at all. One university cancelled on the grounds that the film promotes sexual violence - which was entirely false. A Sydney cinema bowed to pressure from feminists who said the film was evil without having seen it, while a Melbourne venue got death threats for planning to show it. In a final farcical act, someone agreed to show the film, but said the venue would only be revealed twenty minutes before screening. This was to lessen the chance of another mob trying to stop people watching it. As one wit said, 'The all-powerful patriarchy can't assemble openly in public, you know.'

If this is an example of feminism as an 'intellectually and ethically rigorous movement,' let's all have a good laugh at it while it's still legal. And let's stop pretending feminism has anything to do with the search for knowledge, and admit it's just the pursuit of power by angry zealots.

Here are a number of comments left under a YouTube interview with *The Red Pill*'s director, Cassie Jaye:

1. People vastly underestimate the power of 3rd wave feminism. If they don't want you to speak, they have every tool at an institutional level to not only shut you down but destroy your entire life. They are the oppressors and not the oppressed, that is their disguise.

2. (They) are not interested in anything you have to say and just want you shut down. They want to be allowed to do and say whatever they feel but not allow you to do the same if you disagree with them...extremism is dangerous no matter what the issue and you get a bunch of these warriors together and they get that mob mentality going and it's all over.

3. Cassie Jaye is The Poster Child for True Intellectual Honesty, and her journey should absolutely be required study for all college kids today!

4. I can't fault someone for being sucked into a repressive cult. It happens even to decent, sane, educated people.

With the brain-washing and psychological abuse cults perform on their victims, their very thinking processes are completely screwed up. That's why it almost always takes outside intervention from people who aren't indoctrinated into the cult thinking in order to rescue someone who has been brainwashed. It's a rare person who has enough introspection and self-awareness to actually realize that they are in a cult and turn their backs on it.

During the fuss over *The Red Pill*, several people tried to dismiss it as a propaganda film funded by MRAs. This is a cowardly way of trying to brush off your critics. Are they suggesting Cassie Jaye faked her gradual journey from feminism to a more balanced position? If so, Jaye is a remarkable actor. We'd also have to believe the protesters in the film who shut down the MRA meeting were actors paid to portray a mob of fanatics. Yet as we know left wing extremists *do* behave like this, it must have saved some money to just let them show up and do their thing.

Even if the film *had* been financed by MRAs, that wouldn't invalidate it, any more than if a feminist book or film was financed by groups sympathetic to feminism. Yet according to Cassie Jaye herself, the film was funded by 'three generations of feminists' - her mother, grandmother, and herself. When the money ran out in post-production, she turned to crowd-funding and received some money from MRAs. However, when Jaye appeared on an Australian TV show, the interview footage was edited to suggest the film was fully funded by MRAs. The implication was that MRAs had controlled the agenda, tone, and content of the film.

In other words, the TV show used lies and propaganda to suggest that *The Red Pill* was composed of lies and propaganda. It's an example of why the media is less trusted now than at any time in living memory.

If you want to pretend *The Red Pill* is a propaganda film, go ahead. If you want to ban screenings and attack people who show up to watch it, great. But don't go and claim that your movement is in any way 'intellectually and ethically rigorous.'

And the rest of us, be on guard. Big Sister is watching you.

5

The Evil That (Wo)Men Do

Problem 10 - Misogyny and Misandry

Hate. You've gotta love it. It sure makes for some thrilling contests on the sports field. On the field of gender relations, it fuels some vigorous fights as well. Except it isn't a sports field so much as a battlefield, with real dead bodies on each side. Blood, orphans, flowers on coffins...

My guess is that there's rarely been more hatred between men and women than there is now. Sure, there was plenty of anger from women during 1970s second-wave feminism, but today there is actual hate. Not just from women towards men, but from men towards women. There was no MGTOW movement in the seventies. That is, 'Men Going Their Own Way,' boycotting marriage and women altogether.

Feminists will tell you this is because men are bitter at losing their former positions of power over women. They're angry that their 'slaves' have risen up. This is a weak explanation we must go beyond.

The line between anger and hate can be a little blurry. For example, the feminist Clementine Ford is often accused of hating men, a charge she rejects. A man who knows her work might say, 'if Clementine doesn't hate men, I'd sure hate to meet a woman who does.' Still, with some effort, I'm prepared to believe her. Maybe she's just an idealist who thinks people should behave better than they so often do.

Ford's newspaper columns offer an ongoing saga about 'the evil that men do.' They're part of her campaign for a better world. But you'd think from her writing it's only men who do evil. Hasn't she ever watched *Deadly Women* on the crime channel?

In discussing the evil that men do, let us - just for a moment - revert to the sexist language of yesteryear in using the term to include both genders. 'Man,' in that retro sense, is capable of some foul and despicable deeds.

For a window into the evil of which both sexes are capable, read *Divorce Confidential* by G. Nissenbaum. He's a lawyer specialising in divorce among the super rich. The book shows the moral depths either sex can reach in pursuit of their own selfish wants and the wish to hurt others. To go a bit further down the socioeconomic scale, just watch a few episodes of *Judge Judy*. It's the same sort of malice, only more petty.

One of the great things about Judge Judy is she doesn't discriminate on the basis of sex or race. She calls out wrongdoing no matter who is doing it. Clementine Ford, however, usually mentions only the evil done by males. So, for the sake of balance, it's also good to hear from someone like Paul Elam. Elam is the leading men's rights activist in America. For some people, an MRA is to a feminist what a Satanist is to a Christian. They're certainly 'demonised' in mainstream media. Indeed, some writers think just calling someone an MRA is enough to end a debate.

Ford and Elam have a few things in common. Both are outspoken and provocative. They're loved by their supporters and reviled by their detractors. And they're both very angry about the damage inflicted by the opposite gender on their own.

Now, while feminists are happy for Clementine Ford to make her case, they're a lot less keen on Paul Elam making his. Perhaps this is because they still believe the old line about men always getting to speak first, due to their enormous power and privilege. This is odd, because while I get to see Ford's column in my newspaper once or twice every week, I can't recall *ever* seeing one by Elam or any MRA. Indeed, there's such a steady coverage of women's issues in my local paper, *The Sydney Morning Herald*, it may as well change its name to *The Feminist Daily News*.

This imbalance makes you wonder about one of the key feminist beliefs. Isn't it the job of the all-powerful patriarchy to silence women? If so, it really needs to lift its game. In truth, feminism, far from being a small rebel movement, is now part of the establishment. It is Paul Elam's voice which is silenced, not Clementine Ford's.

By the way, Ford's new book contains a direct attack on MRAs and Elam. I'll address that soon. The last chapter of her *previous* book is called 'It's Okay To Be Angry.' Of course, where women have real grievances, they do have a right to be angry. But here's the difference: Ford doesn't think it's OK for *men* to be angry. She belittles MRAs as 'whiny man-babies.' In other words, when women complain, they're freedom fighters; when men complain, they're just whiners.

When both genders face their own problems, why would Clementine Ford treat MRAs with such contempt? She seems to think that compared to women's problems, men's issues are trivial or non-existent. As has been made clear in her writing, Ford thinks women live in a world of pain caused by men, and that our society overall has been set up by men for their own benefit. These ideas form the basis of what I will call Feminism's False Narrative, or the FFN for short.

The FFN

1. All life's suffering goes one way, onto women, caused by men.
2. All the injustice goes one way, against women.
3. Everything is set up in favour of men.

The word 'all' is perhaps an exaggeration. Some feminists admit not *everything* goes in favour of men, and let's not forget the old party line, 'patriarchy hurts men too.' Yet even if, technically, feminists don't believe all life's suffering goes one way, many of them carry on as if they *do* believe it. To concede the point, though, I'll modify the Feminist False Narrative to this:

The FFN

1. Women's suffering is much worse than men's, and most of it is caused by men.
2. Most gender injustice goes one way, against women.
3. Almost everything is set up in favour of men.

We get variations of the FFN each day in feminist-dominated media. It's a focus on either the idea that men's lives are so much easier than women's, or the evil done by men and suffered by women.

The larger context to this is the rise of 'identity politics' - a way of thinking which obsessively defines people in terms of their race, gender, and so on. This might have been relatively benign, but it's always done with a sense of grievance. It's framed as a power struggle, with one group pitted against another.

In this system, white males are seen as the group which oppresses all others, and for whom life is super easy. Indeed, one might think all white males automatically become CEOs when they turn twenty-one. Those who believe this sort of fairytale are almost never white males.

In his brilliant book, *The Victims' Revolution*, Bruce Bawer describes how identity politics has taken over Western universities, teaching students to despise European civilisation and white males. Bawer thinks identity politics leads to a crude and simplistic way of seeing the world. He describes meeting a feminist academic, a Professor Rose:

> According to the mentality of an ideologically orthodox
> academic like Rose, all white bourgeois heterosexual
> men are by definition powerful, while those who are
> non-white, non-heterosexual, and non-male are by
> definition powerless...

> On one level, Rose certainly realizes that as a professor
> at a major university she enjoys a good deal more power
> than most people - white, male, or whatever. But on
> another level she seems honestly to think that she is
> oppressed. So convinced is she of this that it would be
> useless to try to explain to her that this reduction of
> human relations to certain ultra-tidy notions of group
> oppression results in an outrageously crude picture of
> the world ... One might at least try to persuade her that
> plenty of people are oppressed - or ignored, mocked,
> or looked down upon - for reasons other than race,
> class, gender, or sexual orientation. What, for example,
> about the short, old, fat, and unattractive? What about
> those with psychiatric disorders, chronic illnesses,
> physical handicaps, mental retardation? What about
> the bald and bespectacled?

> The list can go on and on. One would think that
> making this point would be a good way of getting
> people like Rose to stop thinking in terms of a handful
> of narrow categories and to look at human experience
> in a more complex, nuanced way, viewing every person
> as an individual and every situation on its own terms.

Let's return to feminism's basic false premise: that most of life's
injustices are suffered by women and everything goes in favour

of men. We should reject this narrative for two main reasons. First, because it is not true, which is reason enough on its own, and second, because of its effect, which is to create a poisonous atmosphere between men and women.

If you could choose one word to sum up the emotional tone of 1970s second-wave feminism, the word might be *anger*. For third-wave feminism, the word would be *hate*. There's a difference.

Hate. It's what misogyny and misandry have in common. Misogynists hate women; misandrists hate men. Some feminists say that while misogyny can be fatal for women, misandry only hurts men's feelings. That's not true. Misandry kills men too, just more indirectly. As for where misogyny comes from in the first place, who knows, but you can bet *misandry* is doing nothing to reduce it.

If third-wave feminism isn't a hate movement, it's certainly the next best thing. Read through most feminist texts and you'll find little in the way of gratitude for anything men do, or sympathy for anything they experience. What you tend to find is a parade of grievance and resentment. This one-sided way of seeing the world is based on the false premise that all life's suffering goes one way, against women, and that all the advantages go the other way, to men.

To disprove this false premise, you need only take one basic area of male-female interaction, which is marriage. If you believe feminist propaganda, men have the advantage in every part of this process. The man is the powerful, privileged leader while the woman is his poor, put-upon junior partner, forced to subordinate her needs to his, acting as a lesser-paid domestic drudge and mother to his children, penalised in her career while he pursues his, and so on. Yes, it sounds like something out of the 1970s, but recent news articles still portray this as the norm.

So, call that a Type One marriage. To be clear, there *are* still marriages like this. While that's not in dispute, we should also admit there are plenty of marriages which are nothing like that at all.

A Type Two marriage is more gynocentric - that is, female centred. It's one where the man, having committed himself to a woman, then subordinates his own needs to her, often compromising his values, interests, and ambitions in order to please her. His life after marriage is based on accommodating his wife's plans, needs, and desires.

There will be some Type One marriages where the man dominates, but there'll be just as many Type Two marriages where the woman does, if perhaps more subtly. While feminists often tell you about the first type of marriage, they rarely mention the second.

To be clear, neither type of marriage is ideal, where one partner has much more power than the other. The point is, it's foolish to suggest all marriages are Type One when there are plenty of Type Twos. Thus, it is also foolish to believe everything in life favours men. To take an even more obvious disproof of the idea, one has only to look at what happens when marriages end.

MRAs believe that the legal system favours women over men in divorce, especially for child custody. Clem Ford disputes this in her book, yet many men certainly believe it. After all, it's one of the main reasons there's a 'marriage strike' and the MGTOW movement. And the *threat* of divorce will also have an effect on marriages themselves. Knowing how badly they are liable to come out of a divorce, many men whose marriages head south realise too late the danger they've put themselves in. This reduces their bargaining power within a marriage. If the wife can always play the divorce card, the husband is less likely to stand his ground on key issues, even if they are important to him.

It's inevitable most marriages involve some politics, a certain 'balance of power' dynamic. When power manifests as control, that is an abuse. It's easy to detect in the case of controlling husbands. They are overt bullies. But there are also plenty of wives who want to control their husbands. Some do it overtly; others more subtly. The latter type are covert bullies.

Men, on the whole, tend to be upfront and rather naive in relationships. If they fall in love with a woman, they love her for who she is. *Some* women love a man for who he might become. The difference is summed up in the phrase 'she hopes he'll change; he hopes she never will.'

In the heady phase of romantic love, these matters often aren't discussed. People forge ahead in a state of blind optimism - and often, one partner changes and the other doesn't. Marriages may decline over time, particularly under the pressure of mortgages and parenting. All too often, people find themselves married to a person who bears little resemblance to the one they married - I mean psychologically, not physically. For one reason or another, marriages fall apart. It happens. But what happens *afterwards* rarely benefits the man.

Of course, women can also be the victims, as with the classic case of the male bastard who trades his faithful wife for a younger woman. Yet as plenty of men also fall victim to emotional entropy, the bastardry goes both ways. The False Feminist Narrative that everything goes in favour of men is not true in marriage, and in plenty of other areas too. Yet the FFN survives.

So what are the fruits of this false narrative? An increase in the *actual* suffering of men. If you keep pushing the lie that everything's in their favour and women are always short changed, you create a poisonous atmosphere in which acts of vindictiveness *seem* justified. You want to destroy some man? Well sure, why not? After all, look at the evil men have done to women. He's one of them, so he deserves it.

It's pretty obvious both genders can be evil. There are plenty of self-serving, parasitical men. There are also plenty of self-serving, parasitical women who will, as Karen Straughan said, 'like looters at a race riot' happily take advantage of laws that discriminate in their favour. They'll keep on doing it right up until their own son, brother, husband, or father is hurt by those same laws.

Let it be clearly understood - a real victim deserves sympathy. Someone who acts the victim while victimising others evokes fury. And as Paul Elam remarked, misogynists are made, not born.

There are several reasons why there is more hatred between men and women than any time in living memory, and the influence of third-wave feminism is certainly among them. Here's what it tends to do:

1. Spreads the FFN that everything goes against women.
2. Stirs up a sense of anger and grievance against men.
3. Ignores any injustices faced by men.
4. Ignores any power and advantages enjoyed by women.
5. Uses the FFN as a reason to push the interests of women and girls, and discriminate against men and boys.
6. And ultimately, creates a climate of hatred that leads to vindictiveness towards men...which in turn leads to resentment against women.

There is a solution to this problem, and that is to abandon the false premise on which all this is based. We should scrap the FFN, and the sooner the better. Unfortunately, many feminists will never give up the idea. If so, they can rest assured that third-wave feminism will continue to be widely disliked and opposed, as it is today.

'He For She'?

Not on those terms.

Real Equality, Real Balance

According to second-wave feminist, Joyce Nicholson, before the Married Women's Property Act of 1870, women forfeited their rights and their money when they married. Their husbands took control of any money and property they may have owned, even if the woman was an heiress with a large fortune. If this is true, we can agree this system was unfair to women and was rightly changed. If you oppose injustice, however, why would you permit a divorce and custody system which is unfair to men today?

It's hard not to see it as some form of revenge. One may wish to right historical wrongs but, once again, we are not a gestalt. There's no connection between individual men of the twenty-first century and those of the nineteenth, just as there is none between women of those eras. Financially eviscerating some man in 2020 is not going to avenge wrongs done in 1820.

The main effect of the FFN has been to create an atmosphere of hate between men and women, which in turn leads to acts of vindictiveness. Misandry doesn't kill men? I'd wager it does, and women too. Stirring up hate between the sexes benefits no one. On an everyday level, misandry also has an effect. A YouTube video by one ex-feminist has an interesting response in the comments.

> My story is similar to yours...I grew up in a very feminist country (Sweden), and have been taught most of my life...that boys are "the bad apples" and the victim mentality was instilled in me at an early age, as

far back as preschool. It was reinforced by my mother, who was married to a narcissist (my father), who not only abused her and me verbally, but was generally, well, a dick (interestingly enough, he was raised by a very self-absorbed, neglectful single mother). So my mother said that "it's just how men are." I grew up believing this, which is ironic, since most of my friends in school were boys, and I've been a tomboy since I can remember. But having the feminist rhetoric and narrative force-fed to me through the school curriculum and media and society in general, I ended up treating my ex boyfriend terribly, *because* he was a man [emphasis added]. For instance, being generally paranoid and mistrustful of him although he never gave me a reason to be, acting entitled like he owed me things, expecting him to do things for me and nag him if he didn't, etc. I cringe, just thinking about it.

A few years ago, I became active on Tumblr, (and) unfortunately, I was "educated" on social justice issues, feminism, "body positivity" and what have you as a side-effect. I started hanging out with a former classmate from high school who also had a Tumblr account, and was a hardcore SJW, and so I started to become more like them. But the more I read her posts...and the more I interacted with her, the more I started to realize that literally everything is always problematic for these people. Nothing ever makes them happy. And it's exhausting! So, naturally, I started questioning if this is a healthy way of living...

Aside from that, I have just always liked to see both sides of a problem...So, one night, I decided to listen to the Anti-Feminist side of YouTube, when I stumbled upon Lauren Southern. To my surprise, I found myself agreeing with most of what she had to say. It led me to Sargon of Akkad, Thunderf00t...Karen Straughan, Honeybadgerradio, etc, and I had a similar "awakening" as you. It dawned on me, essentially, how misguided I had been, and to be honest, what an awful person I had been. I'm really grateful that I was curious and kept an open mind to see "the other side of the problem."

Note the key points in this account:

1. This person was indoctrinated with the idea she was oppressed and men were the problem. This was reinforced through parents, school, the media, and her peers.
2. This caused her to treat her ex-boyfriend terribly *because* he was a man.
3. Eventually she escaped feminist ideology, realising what she'd been taught was not true, or only partly true.
4. Once the indoctrination no longer worked, she realised only in hindsight how it had affected her behaviour, that in some respects, she had been 'an awful person' - not overall, but at least in her treatment of certain other people.

This is an example of how feminism sets up an artificial war between men and women through its divisive ideas. That these ideas are even propagated through schools and universities shows how much institutional power this movement has attained.

This is not to deny there are genuine feminist issues, or that the cause isn't well intentioned. That's why feminism is 'the vast and the spurious.' It's a mix of truth, lies, and opinions. The movement began as a just cause but has become a distortion of what it once was.

This mess may eventually be sorted out, but it will take a while. In the meantime, there will be rival sides with wildly incompatible views. As for the neutrals who are not yet believers, let them hear both sides and make up their own minds. Let the best feminists step up and present their case - but let their critics speak too. By all means listen to the best feminist writers and speakers. But in the interests of balance, also listen to people like Karen Straughan, Janice Fiamengo, Warren Farrell, and even the 'evil' Paul Elam.

Elam is the leading American MRA. He sometimes 'chooses to offend' in his role as men's rights provocateur but don't be fooled by the feminist smear campaign, which includes quotes out of context and other lies. Elam has many interesting things to say in his YouTube talks on *An Ear For Men*. Elam is outspoken, but he found out long ago that calm understatement doesn't work.

Karen Straughan is a brilliant analyst. Listen to some of her recorded talks and you may re-evaluate tales you've been told about the balance of power between men and women. Janice Fiamengo is another woman who offers incisive criticisms.

It's also worth listening to a rogue feminist like Camille Paglia, whose book *Free Women, Free Men* has many moments of brilliance.

As for hardcore feminists, most won't be persuaded by anything I or others might say. Those less committed should reconsider what they've been taught, especially the idea that men have a monopoly on evil and women a monopoly on sorrow. It's bullshit, and simply stirs up hatred between the sexes.

Unfortunately, it is feminists who control the narrative at

present. They assume the right to push their biased view of the world onto naive young minds. During a podcast called 'Happy Father's Day, You Piece of Shit,' Paul Elam said he sometimes hears from fathers who find themselves the target of anger after their daughters have been radicalised into feminism at college.

These are fathers keen to support their daughters' education and career prospects, yet are surprised to find they're actually paying for their daughters to despise them. Elam tells the fathers one solution might be to stop paying the tuition fees, but most are reluctant to do so. 'OK,' Elam replies, 'but if you send your daughter (to university), don't be surprised if she hates your guts when she comes home.'

Hate. You've gotta love it.

6
Fight Fire With Water

The previous chapter was written long before I read *Boys Will Be Boys*, the new book by Clementine Ford. Chapters 6-8 of that book are a blistering attack on her enemies, including men's rights activists (MRAs). Ford is one of Australia's best known modern feminists, with over 100,000 Twitter followers. But as she doesn't seem to understand MRAs, chapters 6-8 of *my* book will try to remedy the false picture of them she gives to her readers.

Doing this means stepping outside the gender war to look at the bigger picture of the 'culture war' which has raged in the West for a while now. This is the battle between the left and right, 'progressives' and conservatives, over the values and direction of Western nations. I'll preface my comments by saying I supported the left side of politics most of my life, until realising what it has become.

People on the right tend to think leftists are mistaken but well meaning. Those on the left think rightists are mistaken and *evil*. Leftists tend to be Utopians who can't understand why anyone would oppose them. Reasonable MRAs would concede that Clementine Ford acts from good intentions, but it's doubtful she'd return the favour.

Ford attacks MRAs in general, and two enemies in particular: Milo Yiannopoulos and Paul Elam. While I certainly don't agree with everything those two say, the point is that you don't have to. The demand for moral purity is a weakness of the left, and barely a week goes by without them hounding someone into oblivion for some social media gaffe, or decades-old *faux pas*. For those on the right, you might not like all of what someone says or does, but still think their views can have value.

Milo Yiannopoulos is a loose cannon who rails against the various holy crusades of the left, including feminism and political correctness. He's part jester, part activist. Ford can't fathom that Milo really does believe his trolling is "God's work." She thinks he's a force for chaotic evil and nihilism. Anyone who's read Milo's book would know that's not true. He has a cruel side to his character, which does him no favours, but it's silly to dismiss him as a nihilist. On the other hand, it *is* nice to see Clementine attacking a non-heterosexual man for a change.

You have to employ a filter with people who act as provocateurs. Filter out Milo's ego and antics and you see an honest activist. Filter out Ford's viciousness and you see a good writer who's trying to create a better world. Look past Elam's click bait headlines and you see a man of rare honesty with an unusual take on gender issues.

Ford's feud with Milo goes back a few years, and most recently to a stunt from his Australian tour when he showed an unflattering picture of her on the big screen for his audience to laugh at. It was a cheap and nasty stunt in which Yiannopoulos played the boarding-school-bully. For this, he was taken to task by right wing pundit, Andrew Bolt, on Bolt's TV show. Milo's defence was, 'the left destroy people. They've been doing it for years.'

While this doesn't excuse his nasty stunt, it's also true. As Ben Shapiro said in his book, *Bullies*, the left routinely set out to destroy people they consider enemies. Just look at a Twitter mob in action. Ford said a proposed debate with Milo would be seen as little more than a 'blood sport' by his fans. She's probably right, but what else is the culture war these days but a blood sport? What else are chapters 6-8 of *Boys Will Be Boys* but an attempt to crush and destroy the so called 'manosphere'? Ford might not criticise MRAs' looks, but she trashes everything else - their character, motives, and intelligence. It's an attempt to shame them into silence or, failing that, to destroy their credibility with the public.

On one hand, you've got to admire Ford's willingness to attack, but her tendency to straw-man her enemies means any victories are mostly imaginary. The next couple of chapters are an attempt to rectify the very partial view of MRAs she presents to her mainstream readership, who will take her words at face value.

Ford doesn't present a fair portrait of MRAs, but a cartoonish distortion based on the various men who abuse her on social media. Apparently, she has received several years worth of personal abuse. That is uncalled for. Clementine Ford is entitled to her views. While others are entitled to answer them, this shouldn't extend to abuse. The men who do this aren't helping their cause. If they think they're striking a blow against feminism with personal insults, they should realise all they're doing is justifying feminists' worldview and giving them ammo.

Then again, it's not as if such abuse has materialised out of thin air. It's possible seven years of Ford's anti-male articles for Fairfax Media might have something to do with it. She also has a provocative persona and seems to relish antagonising men with a special blend of shaming, sarcasm, and condescension. Maybe this persona has been contrived for combat in the gender wars. Or maybe that's just her.

Clementine can also throw a fair insult herself. She left her job at Fairfax after they cautioned her for calling Australia's prime minister a 'fucking disgrace' on Twitter. She also called conservative journalist, Miranda Devine, a cunt on national TV. Not as a term of endearment like Inga Muscio might, but a term of abuse. Seems a wee bit misogynist.

There are also a few pearlers in *Boys Will Be Boys*. MRAs are 'man-babies,' of course. Enemies Mark Latham and Milo

Yiannopoulos get descriptions involving vomit, pus, and other bodily discharges. Milo is not just a regular cunt like Devine, he's a 'massive cunt.' His personality is equated to pig shit, which we must infer is even lower than the human kind.

You might almost start to get a vibe that she doesn't like him.

Ford couldn't understand why the Australian media gave Milo any airtime at all. The answer to that is there's far more to him than the caricature Ford presents in her book. A quick read of 'Middle Rages' shows that. This is an article Milo wrote in defence of Rachel Fulton Brown, a medieval scholar who became a target of the thuggish academic left. Milo's vigorous defence against such bullies is one reason he's so popular.

As for Clementine's insult war, you might say *so what?* Yet it provides a little context for her blistering attack on MRAs. She has set out to destroy them for the edification of her readers. Well, she can come in all guns blazing, but this attack calls for a defence - and the best form of defence is attack. Not that there's much point fighting fire with fire. Water is more effective.

Before doing that, let's give Clementine Ford her due, as it is only fair to respect an adversary. She is a good writer who is sincere in her activism. She has shown the willingness to attack her enemies when plenty of others lack the fortitude. She makes some good points in her writing, and does combat some real problems. Ford should be allowed to make her case, and does not deserve most of the vitriol she has received on social media.

Having said that, her combative persona has annoyed many people. She has converted a few to feminism, and also made plenty into MRAs. She's a provocateur who has successfully antagonised many people - including myself into writing this chapter!

That is all well and good, but her false portrayal of MRAs

should not pass unchallenged. As long ago as 2015, anti-feminist Karen Straughan pointed out that feminists have three main modes of attacking MRAs: first, ridicule; second, the pretence that MRAs are knuckle dragging bigots who pose a threat to civilisation; and third, a further pretence it is really *feminists* who are helping men with their issues, so MRAs should defer to their wisdom. All three are an attempt to make MRAs shut up, or to stop others listening to them. Straughan's talk on this ('An Open Response to SFU's Feminist Constituency') is worth a listen.

Ford employs all three modes in her attack on MRAs. But the real problem is she doesn't understand how MRAs think. Before explaining this, I'll start by trying to understand how people like *her* think.

Patriarchy and The Glorious Revolution

Feminists believe we live in a social system called patriarchy which divides people into two genders, male and female. Individuals are conditioned to think and behave in certain ways depending on which group they're in. This overly strict system is harmful to everybody, including men, but mainly to women, who are placed in lesser roles. Patriarchy heavily favours men, giving them privileged status and the right to dominate. Under these conditions, masculinity can turn 'toxic' when men abuse their power against women.

According to feminists, neither patriarchy or masculinity are natural. They are simply ideas that have been used to construct our society. Therefore, if we could only see, understand, and dismantle these artificial ideas, we can create a more equal society where both men and women are far better off.

This is what I will call 'the Glorious Revolution.' The idea is that once patriarchy is destroyed, everyone will be equal. But the revolution isn't just about gender, it's also about race. In that version, whites take the villain role, and 'whiteness' equates to patriarchy. Whiteness is a system of power which subjugates non-whites.

There are other types of dominance too, like heterosexuality over homosexuality. It's all part of what feminists call 'intersectionality.' Various types of oppression combine. In light of this, it's easy to see why straight white males are the most reviled demographic for leftist revolutionaries.

Until recently, I didn't understand why leftists are so interested in transgender issues. Of course, it's all about weakening the idea of gender itself; of breaking down the 'gender binary' which formerly defined everyone as either male or female. This is part of the war on patriarchy.

Clem Ford says that 'we all have a role to play in dismantling the twin towers of homophobia and misogyny.' It's a strange choice of image. Of course, the main thrust of her work is about taking down only one of those towers. Still, you can only fly one plane at a time.

Those who believe in the Glorious Revolution often struggle to understand why anyone would oppose them. Why would anyone not want to make a better world? Ford notes that MRAs are strangely reluctant to join the revolution, and thinks they are only harming themselves. MRAs 'are capable of recognising the harm that patriarchy does to men...but instead of working with feminists to dismantle this system of structural oppression, they've identified women as its source.'

Well, that's one theory; here's another. One of the main reasons MRAs haven't joined the revolution is they have a fundamentally different view of the world. They don't think their problems are caused by *patriarchy*. They don't see society as patriarchal to begin with, they see it as 'gynocentric.' While feminists see lots of misogyny, MRAs see plenty of misandry.

Where feminists focus on the evil that men do, MRAs' interest is in the under-reported female version.

Ford believes misogyny is rampant under patriarchy and men are revered. MRAs certainly don't think men are revered. Nor do they think most men are powerful. Warren Farrell's 1993 book *The Myth of Male Power* is a seminal text for them.

MRAs don't see the theory of patriarchy as self evident fact the way feminists do. They propose a counter theory that society is actually 'gynocentric' in that, in some ways, it favours and revolves around the interests of women. Men are 'disposable.' I won't get into a discussion of that here, but for those open minded enough to consider it, the theory of gynocentrism is a fascinating alternative to the idea of patriarchy. Both theories are probably too extreme. At the end of the day, the truth lies somewhere in the middle - and no amount of eye-rolling from feminists is going to change that.

Problems With Ford's Portrayal of MRAs

Three of the main problems with Ford's view of MRAs are as follows. First, she treats different types of 'anti-feminists' as if they're all the same. Second, she has contempt for them and tends to straw-man them (that is, she presents a caricature rather than a fair portrayal). And third, she doesn't understand their motivations.

1 - Confusing Different Types

The so called 'manosphere' is made up of various types of men who tend to oppose feminism. While Ford does discuss them separately, she seems to think they're all much the same. When she offers her most damning comments on these people, she refers to 'MRAs,' implying that all anti-feminists are MRAs. She tends to lump together MGTOW (men going their own way), PUAs (pick up artists), 'incels' (involuntary celibates), and MRAs (men's rights activists). These groups are hardly the same. While PUAs may want to pick up women, MGTOW just want nothing to do with them - a male version of the 1970s female separatists.

Incels are an unfortunate group of young men who can't find girlfriends. A small percentage turn their frustration into acts of violence against women, Elliot Rodger being a well-known example. Yet some feminists imply Rodger is representative of MRAs in general.

In similar fashion, a character like Roosh V is mistakenly equated with Paul Elam. Elam has publicly disavowed Roosh and his Return of Kings website. As Ford herself notes, neither does Roosh V call himself an MRA - yet in the same passage, she falsely attributes his values to MRAs.

> Roosh is not an outlier in the MRA world, even though he publicly distances himself from the movement. The belief that men have been stripped of their natural roles as 'leaders' (and the rewards that come with it, which always, *always* include access to nubile young women's bodies) is fundamental to the MRA philosophy.

This statement shows that Ford doesn't understand MRAs and is working from a fictional idea of what they are. Sadly, most of her readers will take her words at face value.

Given that the current chapter is a defence of MRAs, I had better be clear on what I mean by the term. I'm referring mainly to the sort of material found on *A Voice For Men*, the main American MRA website, and the YouTube talks by the likes of Janice Fiamengo, Karen Straughan, and Paul Elam. (Having heard many talks by these three, I can't recall anything about men as leaders, or nubile young women). I'm not very familiar with Roosh V so I am not defending him. Nor am

I discussing pick up artists, incels, MGTOW, or the various people who post on 4chan or Reddit.

In spite of their differences, Clementine Ford seems to think all these people are much the same. Here's how she describes the 'manosphere.'

> Drawing together users from 4chan, 8chan, Reddit, YouTube, Twitter, Facebook, independently run blogs and the sewerage pipes that connect the lot of them, the vast toilet system that makes up this manosphere can be accurately summarised by three words: angry, paranoid, and entitled.

2 – Contempt For MRAs

This brings us to the second main problem with Ford's relationship with MRAs - her contempt for them and desire to convey this to the world. To be fair, many of the people she attacks are equally contemptuous of feminism, so it's no wonder she sees them as enemies. After all, they would say 'angry, paranoid, and entitled' is a perfect description of feminists. Still, the following cavalier dismissal of MRAs gives some idea of Ford's stance.

> Unlike the feminist movement, which throughout its rich and storied history has sought to liberate all humans from the oppressive structures of patriarchy, the men's rights movement is founded on the basic conviction that women are trying to fuck men's shit up and it isn't fair.

This remark, intended as humour, sums up Ford's attitude: the reverence for feminism as a holy cause and the contempt for MRAs, along with a crude misrepresentation of their position.

At this point, we might recall her surprise that MRAs don't want to work together with feminists to solve society's problems.

Ford presents a superficial look at MRAs' concerns, written from a standpoint of pure antagonism. Yet presumably her readers are meant to take her words as gospel. Like many on the left, Ford portrays her enemies as stupid or evil and thinks that is sufficient grounds to dismiss them. But any readers with an interest in how MRAs actually think will find few answers in *Boys Will Be Boys*.

3 - False Understanding of MRAs' Motivations

In looking at Ford's views on the motivations of MRAs, we should remember she seems to confuse them with MGTOW, PUA, incels, and Milo Yiannopoulos fans. With that in mind, she thinks 'MRAs' can be understood as rampant misogynists upset by the loss of their power over women, a loss they want to amend as soon as possible. Mind you, this is not to single out Ford. Many other feminists hold the same sort of views, which is why paranoid fantasy, *The Handmaid's Tale*, is such a hit.

If I've read *Boys Will Be Boys* right, Ford thinks MRAs' behaviour stems from three main factors: men's desire for power over women, their anger that this power has been taken away, and a basic fear of change. Ford thinks those in the manosphere have been raised with expectations of having power over women. 'They have been successfully conditioned by the patriarchal lie that says 'real men' are defined by their ability to dominate others.'

It follows that their opposition to feminism is because, in liberating women, feminists have robbed men of their power. We are seeing 'the frustrations of men who feel they've somehow been denied all that was promised to them.'

What are these alleged promises? As someone who grew

up as long ago as the 1970s, I can't recall ever having a sense of being 'promised' power over women, nor of wanting it in the first place. Perhaps my upbringing was different to other people's, but I can't remember even an implication of such a thing. One gets the sense Ford is giving us cartoon villains in a fictional world viewed through the lens of feminist ideology. In relation to family court disputes, for instance, she thinks we are seeing 'the indulgence of the MRA male victim mentality, which is really just outrage at being suddenly unable to demand total obedience from family members they consider their lowly subjects.'

According to Ford, MRAs are driven by the desire to grind women into servitude, as we can see in the following passage.

(T)he men's rights movement itself is less about equality between the sexes than it is about maintaining power and privilege over women...

And here we come to the heart of the MRA agenda. It isn't to liberate men from the systems that, among other things, cause them to die earlier, to suffer in silence from debilitating mental health issues, to be denied the opportunities to express their emotional selves. Their agenda is to force women in the process of liberation back into the subservient roles that make all of patriarchy's negative consequences for men easier to bear. Rather than look inwards to see how men can strive for a similar autonomy and independence - one that doesn't, for example, involve women working as unpaid domestic maids for them, raising their children, cleaning their houses, cooking their food and servicing their dicks - they instead lash out, believing themselves to be oppressed.

This is about fear, pure and simple. The men who are drawn to the MRA movement see women's liberation as an assault on their fundamental right to power. They may not be able to compete with other men in that hierarchy, but now they can no longer even assert themselves as superior to the women in their lives. As a result, they resent us, they're afraid of us and they work as hard as they can to punish us for making them feel emasculated and weak.

We can see the same faulty diagnosis in the wider context of the culture war. Ford thinks the reason so many young white men oppose the Glorious Revolution is because they can't stand the thought of equality. The fans of Milo Yiannopoulos, for example, are

> ...young men who feel themselves forced to watch as the world they thought they had been promised steadily slips away - a world where men have dominion over women, where white people have dominion over people of colour, heterosexuals over queer people, and so on and so forth.

So there you have it. Clementine Ford seems to think MRAs, and men in general, are driven by misogyny, resentment, and the desire to dominate women and other 'victim groups.' While this cartoonish portrayal will make sense to those who share her view of the world, it is a false depiction of MRAs that does them a disservice. Still, they are used to that.

While I did not set out to critique Clementine Ford, she has chosen to give a damning assessment of MRAs in her book. Although I'm critical of her views, my chapters are far milder in tone than the corresponding chapters in her book, in which she makes a scorched earth assault on MRAs and tries to blast them into oblivion.

Such an attack invites a defence. Ford is a popular author and has a wide influence - and her readers deserve to hear another side of the story.

Perhaps in time Clementine may come to realise she was wrong about MRAs and revise her views. Given the viciousness of the culture war, you wouldn't bet on it. But who knows? Hell may indeed freeze over, and fire and water may one day reach an unlikely alignment.

7

Resisting the Glorious Revolution

Leftists often fail to understand their opponents' motivations. Because their own ideals seem so self-evidently good, they tend to assign sinister motives to those who oppose them.

Judging by her books, Clementine Ford seems to think MRAs have no greater motivation than the desire for power over women. That's wrong, and a serious misrepresentation of MRAs. Having said that, there *are* some men who think like that, who *do* desire power over women, but I don't think they have much in common with the type of MRAs I am discussing. In, say, the YouTube talks by Fiamengo, Straughan, or Elam, there is very little about men's desire to control women.

It's not true to say all MRAs are on the political right, but many are driven there. If feminism is on the left, those who don't like it will drift right. The left these days has some dubious beliefs, and shows a liking for censorship and other authoritarian traits. It's why many former leftists no longer want anything to do with them.

If feminists really want to understand why people don't support them, they need to go beyond the idea that their opponents are evil. If the left in general want to understand why some of its former supporters have gone away, they should stop dismissing them as racists, Nazis, and so on, as if this is some kind of persuasive argument.

Consider the rise of the so called Alt-Right. Leftists often seem surprised that this movement emerged. They also point to its popularity with white males, as if this is damning evidence against it. Here's a wild speculation on why that might be. Could it be because identity politics has decided white males are the root of all evil and public enemy number one? How astonishing, then, that a movement that's risen against identity politics is attractive to white males.

Other such 'right wing' trends have also emerged, and almost entirely in reaction to the political left. Contrary to leftist belief, white males don't go to the right through a desire to dominate others. They go as a rejection of the idea that their own demographic can be made the target of institutionally endorsed hatred. They go in protest against the rank hypocrisy of the left, whose holy crusade against racism and sexism includes targeting white males on the basis of their race and gender.

Some would say this is overly paranoid - but it is not *these* people who believe *The Handmaid's Tale* is practically a documentary.

Why do young white males go to Milo Yiannopoulos shows? Clem Ford thinks it's because they're angry they don't get to dominate women, people of colour, and homosexuals. It's more likely they go in response to having their own demographic singled out and attacked. They don't believe in the left's Glorious Revolution in the first place, and they don't think the revolutionaries could make a better world anyway. The left may imagine a wonderful place where all races and genders live in equality. But there has been far too much hatred and self interest on display to think any kind of harmony is going to magically appear if the revolution ever comes to pass.

This isn't the place to discuss movements like the Alt-Right in detail, but it's interesting to compare the left's attitude to the Alt-Right and Islam. We already know Ford thinks Milo is morally bankrupt, a force for chaotic evil, and has scandalous links to the far right - but apparently he's also 'Islamophobic.' To which Milo might reply *'Yes, and why aren't you?'* especially given Ford's stance on fighting homophobia. As a gay man, Milo is concerned about the growing influence of Islam in the

West and knows that in *some* Islamic countries, homosexuals are jailed or thrown off buildings. As for the status of women in the more fundamentalist nations, put it this way: if you like Western patriarchy, you'll *love* the new version if the Caliphate ever comes into power.

Apparently, the so called 'far right' is the worst thing in the world if it involves white people, and good leftists should oppose it with all their might. But if *actual* far right values are held by a non-white culture, you must never oppose them and anyone who does is a racist.

It's sad when not everyone shares your values. Sweden has been one of the world's most feminist and progressive countries, and recently put its ideals into practice by welcoming large numbers of refugees. It's rumoured this generous act has had unforseen side effects for Sweden's women, but that's another story. We'd better get back to the real villains, those evil white MRAs.

MRAs

When I began writing this book two years ago, I had never heard of men's rights activists. Since then, I've read articles on the main MRA website, *A Voice For Men*, and listened to many YouTube talks by the likes of Fiamengo, Straughan, and Elam. Based on this, my view is that Clem Ford's depiction of MRAs is well wide of the mark.

If there are old style misogynists out there who want to control women, I would never endorse their views. Yet that sort of mentality has little to do with men's rights activism, as I have observed it so far.

The idea that MRAs are wannabe patriarchs champing at the bit to enslave women is *Handmaid's Tale* paranoia. Mind you, have I not just insinuated the same idea in relation to fundamentalist Islamic countries? Yes, but as that's how some of those countries actually work, it has some basis in reality.

Western feminists have a bizarre fixation on white males as the source of all evil. For example, in an attempt to be fair, Ford notes that some men have been falsely accused of rape and suffered as a result - but she can't help but throw in a racial disclaimer.

> None of this is to say that women don't ever lie about being raped or are incapable of such duplicity. There are circumstances in which people's lives have indeed been destroyed by false allegations or convictions, and there are people who have served incomprehensibly long prison sentences for sexual crimes they were later discovered not to have committed (but it's worth pointing out this is infinitely more likely to happen to men of colour than to white men.)

Oh the agony of showing sympathy for white men! The compassion doesn't even last to the end of the sentence. She has to throw in a *don't think I'm talking about you* in brackets. Thanks a lot.

Now, what feminists write one percent of the time in the pretence of being fair, MRAs take as their main focus. They want a more realistic view of human nature. To echo a famous feminist mantra, MRAs believe in the revolutionary idea that women are people too. That is, people with the capacity for good and evil. If MRAs tend to focus on the evil, it's mainly because it is so under-reported.

Ford mentions a few issues that concern MRAs: paternity fraud, custody rights, and so on. In typical fashion, her treatment of them is cursory and dripping with scorn, to the extent that you wonder if she's playing the troll à la Milo Yiannopoulos. There's even a YouTube video which compares Ford and Milo as two sides of the same coin, speculating that her writing style is intended to make people angry. If so, she must be congratulated on a job well done! Here's one example:

> Ironically, in addition to denying loving dads the right to see their kids, feminism is also responsible for forcing men to become dads in the first place and extorting them for child support they don't want to pay and probably aren't even responsible for because paternity fraud is also A Big Problem according to the charter of paranoid man-babies. Don't be alarmed if you find it confusing; MRAs make sense to nobody but themselves.

Such contempt may be convincing to her supporters, but all she's done is take a few separate issues and stick them together. Note the sleight of hand in the following passage.

> While we're at it, can we all agree that it's a curious bit of cognitive dissonance to argue against paying to support children you don't want in one breath while ranting about how the legal system helps women steal them from you in the other?

The first part of this refers to a woman going ahead with a pregnancy against the father's wishes (presumably unplanned and outside marriage). The second is about another father given limited or no access to his already-born children after a divorce. They are two different men, yet Ford treats them as if they are the same man who just can't make up his mind. Yes, that straw MRA *is* a bit of a laughing stock. Here's a parallel version. How about that woman who wants an abortion and also wants custody of the kid? Oh the cognitive dissonance!

Then again, perhaps Ford is referring to a father who is

unhappy about paying child support for a child he's not allowed to see. If so, we must rack our brains trying to understand the man's attitude. I mean, why would a dad denied access to his kids not want to pay child support? It would be like not having your cake and not eating it. What a fantastic deal.

MRAs tend be annoyed by feminists' portrayal of women as always sinned against, never sinning. Women are as capable as men of evil. They tend to be more underhand about it, but it is evil just the same. Here are two recent examples. What's striking is they contain no outward aggression, are completely covert, but are profoundly evil in robbing their male victims of what was most important to them.

In one case, a woman deceived her husband about the paternity of her three sons, until the boys were grown up. The husband only found out by accident when some medical tests showed he could not be the father. He realised, in hindsight, that the most important relationships in his life were based on a lie.

In the second case, a young man who wanted to be a professional clarinettist got an offer to study with the world's leading clarinet teacher, a man he idolised. Unfortunately, he didn't find out until years later, because his girlfriend rejected it on his behalf using a fake email address. Why? Because she didn't want him to leave town as she feared this might end their relationship. In other words, she sabotaged his deepest dream for the sake of her own selfish desires. They soon broke up anyway. Years later, he found out about the scholarship when he met the idolised teacher, who asked why he'd turned him down.

These two covert crimes were done purely for these women's convenience. If gynocentrism entails the idea that men's worth is in what they can do for women, the crimes were gynocentrism in action. Issues of paternity, parental rights, and general misandry matter to MRAs. Ford can trivialise these issues if she likes, but they aren't trivial to the men who experience them. MRAs don't want to dominate women. They want to challenge the false idea that both power and evil belong exclusively to men.

In a sense, MRAs may be doing more for equality than feminists, for they want women to be seen as full human beings, honest and accountable, rather than infantilized beings who can blame any problem on external factors. In taking a more realistic view of human nature, MRAs may have a better chance of fixing social problems. Let's take domestic violence, for example.

An Alternative Look at Domestic Violence

In her book, Ford tries to do a hatchet job on leading MRA, Paul Elam. Indeed, it is an attack of such vehemence Elam may have felt the thought waves from his home 15,000 miles away. It's utterly one-sided, of course, and anyone interested in the real Paul Elam should go to the source and listen to his YouTube talks and read his articles.

As a sign of his wickedness, Ford quotes the title of one of Elam's talks, 'How to Get Your Man to Punch You in the Face.' She mentions that Elam's talk is about 'relational aggression,' but doesn't tell her readers what that is. As Ford omitted key details from her account, I'll try to fill in the gaps.

Elam sometimes uses provocative titles as 'click bait' without expecting them to be taken seriously. A bit like when Clementine tweeted 'Kill all men' as a joke. Elam's talk was on domestic violence, a contentious topic in the gender wars. Feminists like to pretend domestic violence is all male-on-female, with any female aggression purely in self defence. In her book, Ford refers to 'a reciprocally violent relationship (i.e.

women responding to violence perpetrated against them.)' In other words, she seems to think any violence in a mutually violent relationship has been initiated by the man. This fictional idea of human nature is the sort of thing MRAs try to combat.

Elam's talk is on relational aggression, a covert form of abuse that has been described as 'bullying without violence.' Often associated with teenage girls, it can take the form of excluding, ignoring, spreading rumours, hostile body language, and verbal putdowns. Any woman who was ever bullied in school knows about this. It's not much of a stretch to see this sort of behaviour extending to adult relationships. Elam quotes Erin Pizzey's view that some women act as 'emotional terrorists.' Pizzey ran a domestic violence shelter in England in the 1970s, but was harassed by feminists who objected to her saying both genders are violent.

While men's aggression is more direct, the covert, passive aggression of some women also does harm. In some cases, it can play a part in leading to domestic violence. That doesn't mean the violence is justified, but if the goal is stopping it we should look at all possible causes.

This is almost a test case for comparing patriarchy theory with gynocentric theory in trying to solve a real world problem. Patriarchy theory tells us domestic violence is caused by structural oppression. *Men have power over women, and hit them when they disobey.* It's a simple, one dimensional view of human psychology. (Mind you, the Duluth model for domestic violence, favoured by feminists, does include relational aggression.)

A gynocentric theory of domestic violence also deals with ideas of power, but in a more subtle way. Paul Elam gives a talk called 'When Harry Hit Mary' in which he discusses two main types of men who engage in domestic violence. The first is your standard bully, who fits the stereotype of the petty tyrant within the home. Yes, of course, such types do exist. Elam has little to say about such a guy, 'except that he's an asshole.' (Odd - according to feminists, shouldn't Paul be cheering him on?)

The second type of man faces a different power dynamic. Elam tells a story of 'Harry' and 'Mary' who begin a serious relationship. Mary wants to pair with Harry, but on her own terms. The two get together in a blaze of passion, but she soon begins a gradual process of changing him, playing the sculptor to mold him into her ideal partner. She shaves a bit here, whittles a bit there, polishing and shaping Harry into the desired form.

Harry is like a dog being trained, and he's a bit *too* agreeable. Good natured as a puppy and rather naive, Harry has indeed been socialised into a gender role. Not to dominate women, as patriarchy theory would have it, but to please and serve them, as gynocentric theory says is at least as common.

In between Harry's wish to please and Mary's skill as a sculptor, he gradually changes into something he is not, someone Mary has created. Harry allows himself to be controlled, ignoring the inner protesting voices. He's an abuse victim, yet subtly so, shaped by a thousand small cuts of control. And why would Mary stop? Harry's too out of touch with his feelings to complain, perhaps too inarticulate to form the words. Mary may not even realise part of Harry is silently protesting - until he finally snaps and commits a clumsy act of violence.

This does not mean Mary deserves to be hit or the act is justified. It's simply a look at how such a situation might build up. Harry is to blame for not standing up for himself earlier, but you might also wonder why Mary felt entitled to control him in the first place. And as Elam says, 'who has the power in this scenario?'

This sort of idea will be familiar to feminists, but with the genders reversed - the compliant wife who submits to years of control by a domineering husband, before finally snapping with an act of violence. There are many such cases yet the victims and abusers come in both genders. The standard Duluth model of domestic violence includes forms of relational aggression - but if we're honest, several of these (e.g. emotional abuse, denying and blaming, using children) are likely practised at least as much by women as by men.

In a way, feminists are right that domestic violence may be about power and domination, but in Harry's case, it is a response to it rather than its enactment. To repeat, this doesn't excuse his violence. Elam's talk is simply an attempt to see why a man not violent by nature might commit a violent act. He's been driven towards it via the erosion of his identity by a woman's gynocentric desire to mold him into a servant.

If we're serious about stopping domestic violence, we should dispense with the fiction that abuse only goes one way. In light of this, gynocentric theory may be at least as useful as patriarchy theory in understanding the problem. Elam's *A Voice For Men* website offers a useful alternative to a feminist view of life.

Paul Elam isn't to everyone's taste. He sometimes comes across as too harsh, or overly cynical, but he's prepared to call out feminist lies and the dark side of female nature, and he doesn't give a damn about the flak this attracts. He may have once, but those days are long gone.

Many people find this unnerving. This is what the political left hates - someone who won't be cowed into obeying the party line on how to think. Some people have a lot invested in the Men-Bad-Women-Good narrative, and they've plenty to lose by Elam's debunking of this convenient fiction. Others will find it a refreshing change from the propaganda they normally hear.

Returning to the bigger picture of the left's Glorious Revolution, I'd guess that many MRAs find themselves resisting it almost by accident. They don't do it because they're members of an embattled ruling class. They're responding as members of a class that has been falsely named the enemy.

Neither is the revolution all that glorious. At least, not if you judge it by the revolutionaries. The way they conduct themselves - their ethics, their reasoning, their petty vendettas - is far from grand. One day they may finally realise why people don't support their revolution. They're correct that it's because one side of the culture war is being fought by fascists. Their mistake is not realising which side that is. Perhaps light will eventually dawn and both sides can come together in greater understanding. If not, the culture war will rage until doomsday.

8

Gaslighting the Gender Wars

Kinokuniya is Sydney's largest bookshop, and its Gender Studies section has a lot of feminist books. While some might discuss internal disputes like, say, the status of trans-women, there won't be many critical of feminism itself. You won't find any by MRAs, not even Warren Farrell's *The Myth of Male Power*. Sure, there are far fewer such books in existence, but let's not have any illusions about which side of the gender wars has the 'institutional power.' Gender studies = feminism. Or so they think.

Thanks to support from universities and the media, there have been thousands of books, articles, and courses promoting a feminist view of the world. To be fair, it's easy to see why such a view seems plausible. You can make a good case for it. Books by authors like Soraya Chemaly, Inga Muscio, Laura Bates, bell hooks, and others make a strong case.

The problem is that these books are so focused on one view of the world that other ways of seeing it don't appear in them. This in turn has a hypnotic effect on the reader. There's no doubt a feminist view of the world seems compelling to those immersed in that literature. After all, there's plenty of evidence that seems to support it. There *are* some sexist attitudes. Men *do* enjoy some advantages over women. There *are* less female CEOs. Sexual assault and harassment *are* realities women have to consider. All of this makes feminism quite convincing to those who focus on the supporting evidence and ignore everything else.

In light of that, thank God for alleged 'propaganda film' *The Red Pill*. Let's hope there's more propaganda to come. The film's title is a *Matrix* reference which means waking up from a shared mass illusion. The blue pill view of life is the feminist one we've all semi-consciously absorbed. Because we're so immersed in it, it's a relief to get 'red-pilled' by Karen Straughan or Janice Fiamengo. It's why we accept Paul Elam's occasional harsh words, because it's refreshing to hear someone call out the dark side of female nature.

Still, it's no wonder feminists have little interest in challenges to their worldview, for they have a great deal invested in it. Any other way of seeing the world doesn't have much value, or is seen as a threat. Some of them may be academics but they're also activists.

This is not the way intellectuals are supposed to think, especially scientists and philosophers. There's an odd term that's crept into recent debate - 'gaslighting.' When you argue with a leftist, you may be accused of trying to 'gaslight' them. This has a sinister meaning, for to gaslight someone is to try to make them doubt their perception of reality.

In the olden days of about twenty years ago, this was actually seen as a virtue. A 1997 book by scientist Carl Sagan spoke of the vital importance of gaslighting - except, of course, he didn't use that term. He said that for scientists (or anyone trying to find the truth), self doubt was both noble and necessary. Although it can be upsetting, you have to ask if your theories about the world could be wrong. We should *all* try to gaslight ourselves from time to time as a test for possible delusion.

Universities used to teach critical thinking. They still teach a *type* of critical thinking, which is teaching students to criticise patriarchy, male privilege, and other forms of 'structural oppression.' This is not so much teaching people to think as it is indoctrinating them into supporting the Glorious Revolution. When Milo Yiannopoulos went on his 'Dangerous Faggot' tour of US universities, he was trying to gaslight students into doubting that indoctrination.

Gaslighting in this sense should be a virtue, or at least a useful check on the possibility one may be wrong. When MRAs write about society being gynocentric, they're trying to gaslight those with the conviction it is strictly patriarchal. When Janice Fiamengo criticises feminism, she's trying to gaslight those who've been given a one-sided education on how the world works.

It's understandable feminists have no interest in ideas which threaten their worldview. Some have built their whole identity or career around it. Still, you have to wonder if it actually makes them happy to believe in the patriarchy, male privilege, and the rest of that whole belief system.

Feminists can hate MRAs if they want to. They can pretend MRAs are slavering Neanderthals whose only reason to resist the Glorious Revolution is their desire to enslave women. Other people not so committed should expose themselves to different ways of seeing the world.

To her credit, unlike some other Australian feminists, Clementine Ford didn't call for the banning of *The Red Pill* film. She said it should be screened as an absurdist comedy. Neutrals should call her bluff and actually watch it. They should also consider the views of her other dastardly foes - including the awful Milo Yiannopoulos and the evil Paul Elam. Let's listen to Straughan and Fiamengo, and rogue feminists like Camille Paglia. At the same time, read Ford's books and the best books by other feminists. We should all try to gaslight each other's perceptions of reality, and may the best survive.

If feminist theory is actually true, it should be tough enough to beat off all challengers. If it's only half true, why not keep the good stuff and dump the rest? Maybe a truer view of life is a mixture of patriarchy theory and gynocentrism theory.

Even if feminists were actually right that Western civilisation has been patriarchal, you can't say patriarchy is the worst system, given it has apparently created the modern world. Feminists often tell men to check the unearned privilege they enjoy. Perhaps they should do the same. In those terms, 'patriarchy' has given them the computers they use, the internet they communicate on, the universities at which they work, and the planes in which they travel to their academic conferences. Even if they do believe in the patriarchy, maybe they should consider all they have gained from it rather than seeing it as a giant foot crushing them.

When it comes to defining the state of gender relations, feminism has had a monopoly on the whole racket for the last fifty years. It's surely time for some major gaslighting, some alternate ways of viewing social life. There may even be a few feminists prepared to challenge their beliefs. Some of them might come to realise they're not as oppressed as they thought. Or at least no more oppressed than anyone else. And - who knows - maybe that's good news after all.

9

The Two Hundred Dollar Coffee

Problem 11 - The Gender Pay Gap

One day late in 2017, I walked into a cafe with a female friend. On the table was a newspaper with a headline about TV host, Lisa Wilkinson. She'd just quit her job over being paid less than her male colleague, Karl Stefanovic. Lisa was said to be on about $1.2 million a year while Karl was on two million. She protested by signing with another network who agreed to pay her the same as Karl.

My friend, who is a feminist, pointed to the headline with a look of approval. I got the sense I was meant to be thrilled, that perhaps I should jump up with a cry of solidarity and proclaim, 'Hoorah! The patriarchy is no longer oppressing Lisa Wilkinson!'

Instead, I sat down and ordered a coffee, wondering why I should care about someone on a wage thirty or forty times my own being given a pay rise. Still, maybe I wasn't seeing the bigger picture. Sensing my lack of joy, my friend asked, 'Don't you want your wife to earn the same as the men in her company?' 'She already does,' I replied. 'It was legislated years ago.'

In other words my friend, an intelligent woman, had been so assailed by propaganda about the 'gender pay gap' that she believed my wife is paid less than her male colleagues, despite the Equal Pay Act having been passed in 1963. In most ordinary jobs, it is illegal not to pay men and women the same wage for the same work.

Naturally, this doesn't apply to all professions. Anyone in the entertainment field, for instance, is going to negotiate whatever wage they can get. The footballer, Ronaldo, just signed with

Juventus for fifty million Euros a year. It's just possible there's a small wage gap between him and his team-mates.

There's no such thing as an Equal Pay Act in the entertainment world. In 2015, the actress Jennifer Lawrence was peeved to find out she earned less than her male co-stars for the film *American Hustle*. She still made fifty million dollars from the *Hunger Games* series that year, and was aware enough to know it wasn't a third world problem. Otherwise you might say that anyone - male or female - who is on fifty million and complains about money should be instantly struck by lightning.

Back in the world of mortals like Lisa Wilkinson and me, let's imagine I was in a different cafe - that one in Melbourne which charges men a 17% surcharge to reflect the gender pay gap. And what is this famous pay gap anyway? Well, if you take *all* the men and women who are working full time and compare their income, women are paid, on average, 17% less than men. As a protest, this Melbourne cafe has taken a stand on the issue by charging their male customers 17% more. So, if I ordered a coffee which is normally $4.00, I'd be charged $4.68.

Now suppose Lisa Wilkinson was sitting at the next table. She'd only pay $4.00 for her coffee because she's a victim of the gender pay gap. It's a bit odd when you consider Lisa owns a home in one of the more expensive parts of Sydney, while I'm paying a fair chunk of my salary in rent. Yet this cafe would charge me $4.68 for my coffee and Lisa $4.00 for hers.

I might go up to the justice-minded cafe staff and say, 'I've heard about your income-based prices. If you adjust for our incomes, I'm the one who should pay $4.00 for my cappuccino. Lisa should be charged at least $200 for hers, and if Jen Lawrence or Ronaldo come in, they'll be paying about $10, 000 for theirs.

What this imaginary scene shows is the silliness of identity politics; the absurdity of placing Lisa Wilkinson in a class with all women and myself in a class with all men, and using the single factor of our gender as a basis for policy.

So, on to the topic of the 'gender pay gap' - or the GPG for short. At face value it's the idea that women are ripped off as a class by being paid less than men for the same work. But there's so much more to the GPG debate than that. It's about the gender war in the home and the workplace. It's about who gets to do - or *has* to do - all the work inside and outside the home. Who bears the burden, who reaps the rewards, and which gender gets the overall better deal. As usual, feminists believe women are the ones getting the short end of the stick. Indeed the gender pay gap is one of what I will call the Five Pillars of Feminism.

The Five Pillars of Feminism

1. Male Privilege - that men are automatically better off than women in most areas of life.
2. Patriarchal Control - that women live under social structures that favour men. Women's behaviour is limited by various rules and expectations.
3. Sexism - that women are seen as lesser beings, talked down to, and otherwise not given the same respect as men.
4. Sexual Assault and Harassment - that women face a constant battle against the threat of sexual violence and unwanted attention.
5. The Gender Pay Gap - that women are paid less, discriminated against in the workplace, and forced to do more unpaid domestic labour, which harms their financial power.

There are other contenders for the five pillars. The idea that gender is a social construct is pivotal and should perhaps make the list. Then there's the more recent 'intersectionality,' which is the idea that you can be oppressed in more than one way. But I'll ignore them for now and stick to the classics.

For something as solid as a pillar, the gender pay gap is strangely insubstantial. People can't even agree if it exists in the first place. Some say it's a myth many times debunked. This annoys people like Jessica Valenti, who says it really pisses her off when people say it's not real. Yet mainstream media sure seems to believe in it, judging by how often the topic comes up. Others say the GPG *is* real, but can't agree on whose fault it is. That's probably the better question.

Even if the idea of the pay gap is an illusion, it is quite real in its effects. The gender pay gap, as an idea, is one of the main sources of women's resentment against men. It's the notion that women get a worse deal at work, in the home, and have less social and financial power - all due to systematic forces that favour men. If you believed that, no wonder you would harbour grudges against the male sex.

Some people still can't seem to agree on whether the idea is true or, if it *is* true, what causes it. Either way, the GPG is a problem worth solving. If it's real and women are being discriminated against, it should be fixed. If it's false but belief in the idea is causing undue resentment against men, that should also be fixed.

But you've got to be careful how you do it. A columnist named Louise Roberts wrote a story saying the GPG is real but comes almost entirely from the life choices of individual women. For this she won the 'Least Helpful to the Sisterhood' prize in Australia's annual awards for sexism. That's what you get for denying that the GPG is a crime against women. Yet if they are really serious about ending the pay gap, the only way to do it is from a foundation of honesty - and there's no doubt at all the choices of individual women are one of the main causes of the GPG. There are other factors but that is certainly one. What is *really* Least Helpful to the Sisterhood is lying about what actually causes it.

In the next two chapters, I'll try to solve the problem of the GPG. Yes, I'm going to Help The Sisterhood! Why? Partly to help the brotherhood as well, because the amount of undue rancour and rage directed at men over the GPG does no one any good. Not men, women, or the other thirty-nine genders. Where the GPG is unfair to women, we should remedy it. Where it is unfair to men - in terms of rage, hate, and 'affirmative action' - we should remedy that too. Waging phony wars over phantom oppressions is a waste of time.

Helpful to the Sisterhood? Sure - but the quest to solve the GPG can only begin when we stop lying about what causes it. That's the only way to fix it.

As a simple statistic, the gender pay gap is real. It's the difference between the average earnings of all men and all women working fulltime. It's somewhere between 15-25% difference. When President Obama pandered to women in 2012, he said they earn 77c for every dollar a man earns. Others have said 85c. For the sake of argument, I'll round it to 80c. So if the average man working fulltime earns $50,000, the average woman earns $40,000.

There are some who'll take this literally and think that if, say, McDonalds are paying a teenage boy $10 an hour, they're paying teenage girls $8. That's illegal, and if McDonalds could really do it, they wouldn't be hiring many boys. This is the sort of misunderstanding that results when the raw statistic is used to shame men and stir up women. It leads to ridiculous myths like the idea that women work for free from November to the end of the year.

All too often the stat is taken at face value without looking at the many variables which feed into it. Among them are that men, on average, work longer hours and at higher levels than women. These factors are both consequence and cause of each other. If you work longer hours you tend to rise higher, which in turn makes you work longer hours. Whether or not that's fair is a separate question, but it inflates the wage gap.

One of the key causes of the GPG is that more women choose to train for lower paid professions. On average, men tend to work in higher paid professions (e.g. STEM - science, technology, engineering, and math) and women in lower paid professions (e.g. teaching or social work). To work in these professions one has to train for them, and it 'seems odd' women would deliberately choose to do that. Except, of course, it's not odd at all, because a major false assumption about the GPG is that people choose jobs on salary alone. As everyone knows, there's far more to a choice of career than money. *Everyone* knows this, but strangely forgets it when they talk about the pay gap.

As to why women tend to 'illogically' choose those careers, feminists dislike the idea that many women don't want to do STEM type jobs. It raises doubts about the idea that gender is a social construct, so they tend to argue women are socialised into their life choices. That is, girls are subtly shaped from birth by a great force called Social Expectations into, say, not wanting to study math and science. So if they choose to study teaching, they're not really choosing at all.

There are certainly more women working in STEM now than in the past, but some other fields still have so many women they're sometimes called the 'female professions.' It's not clear why that is, but there's a whiff of conspiracy in the idea women are socialized into choosing to become teachers rather than engineers. What about male teachers - is there a conspiracy against them too? The thing is, there's not just a pay gap between men and women, but between men and men... who work in different professions. What you're really talking about is a Profession Pay Gap. That tends to be overlooked.

You might, however, have a woman and man in the *same* job and she'll earn less over time due to the other main cause of the pay gap - parenting. If she leaves the workforce to become a mother, it harms her career and earnings. Becoming a mother puts her on a lifelong lower trajectory compared to a man. Hence the man's higher level in a company, his ability to work longer hours, and so on, leads to him having more money. This all adds to the wage gap.

There's some truth in this and if this is a problem, the question is who is responsible for fixing it: the woman, her partner, the employer, the government, or the system itself ? These questions will be taken up in the next couple of chapters.

The gender pay gap is a highly misunderstood concept. The 80c stat is given as proof of injustice against women but the actual causes of that stat aren't often explained. Only by being honest about the causes can those women concerned about the pay gap escape it. That is, if there's anything to be escaped from in the first place.

In some ways, that raw stat of 80c is a facade. The real battles of the GPG are about work, inside and outside the home: who gets to do it, who has to do it, and who reaps the rewards. These questions will be discussed in the next chapter.

10

Helpful to the Sisterhood

Fixing the Gender Pay Gap

There are many ways to solve the problem of the gender pay gap. One of the simplest is to realise it is based on a premise that is not only false, but which everyone *knows* is false, which is the idea that money equals happiness. The ultimate goal for most people is to be happy. There are many factors which lead to that state, of which money is only one. If a genie appeared and granted a wish that every adult had exactly the same amount of money, it's absurd to think they'd all be equally happy.

Feminism's ultimate goal may not be to make women happy, but to make them equal to men. But whatever equality actually means, there is far more to it than ensuring the average wage of all women and all men working fulltime is the same. What's more, in trying to achieve that goal, there may be unwelcome side effects for women. Even if they could achieve equal pay, it might not make them happier.

Least Helpful To the Sisterhood

However, if fixing the GPG is a priority for feminism, the advice that's Least Helpful To The Sisterhood is as follows.

Instead of addressing the real causes of the pay gap, women should believe it's a conspiracy by men and the patriarchy. Pretend they have no control over their life choices, then choose to train for lower paid professions. After working for a couple of years, they should marry a man on a higher salary. Then have a couple of kids and complain that, for financial reasons, their husband has to keep working while they have to quit.

Believe that Social Expectations create an all-powerful force blowing women around like motes of dust. Don't forget to reduce complex matters of causality down to a simplistic focus on gender and sexism. Build a state of mind based on grievance and resentment, and keep complaining that *someone should do something*. In other words, keep waiting for that magic genie to appear.

If all of the above is least helpful to solving the GPG, here are some suggestions on what might help.

Action Plan One: Work

It's hard to fathom why someone would train for a profession they know is low paying, then complain about the gender pay gap. Perhaps they weren't told. Then again, people don't choose careers just for the money. They choose them because it's the best option they can think of, or they believe that sort of work will suit their personality. That people don't choose jobs for money alone is something everyone knows, but seems to forget when discussing the GPG.

When choosing a profession, there's always a trade off between doing a job you like and one that pays well. If money is the priority, the simplest step is to train for a high paying job. If doing a job you like is the priority, you train for it anyway and accept the rates of pay. To choose a fulfilling job is honourable. That doesn't mean remuneration is going to bend in your direction.

If money were the only guide, everyone at university would be studying higher paid careers like engineering, IT, or investment banking, and no one would study lower paid careers like teaching or social work. But most people who become teachers or social workers don't have the slightest interest in being engineers or investment bankers. Why should they?

If you're a teacher, you can either accept the pay as it is, or lobby for it to be higher. Some jobs are certainly underpaid. I've tried school teaching myself and whatever they're on, they should double it. It's the job-from-hell, and with what they're expected to do these days, they're not just workers but miracle workers.

Still, there are limits to what can be paid. Shami Chakrabarti says the female-dominated 'caring professions' should be better remunerated (as well as having more men work in them). She asks why investment banking is seen as having such a proportionately greater value than teaching or palliative care.

While she's right about the absurd scale of the imbalance, she must know that teachers will never earn anything like bankers. Presumably, investment banking involves risky manoeuvres with large sums of money in the private sector, while teaching is a public sector job with very different aims. It's hard to compare such different jobs in terms of their 'value.' Their social value has little to do with their financial value. Even if teaching may be more worthwhile, in a sense, that won't translate into wages.

In terms of money alone, the GPG is partly the result of many more women than men choosing to be teachers rather than investment bankers. So, you can pay teachers more, or try to get more women to train for banking careers. Or you can just say, 'that explains the gender pay gap,' and move on.

Action Plan Two – Marriage

One of the main causes of the pay gap is marriage and children. A video on an Australian government website tells the story of 'William' and 'Amelia' who enter the same job equally qualified. After a couple of years, Amelia takes a year off to give birth and raise her child. When she returns to the job part time, William's career has advanced. By the time Amelia reestablishes herself in full time work, William has moved ahead, earning a promotion. When they eventually retire, he'll have earned more and retire with more superannuation. Amelia's career trajectory was harmed by her decision to take a year off for parenting.

The simplistic answer for women deeply troubled by the GPG is to not have children. The more probing questions are whether it should be Amelia's husband taking a year off to care for the baby, or whether the government and employers should be doing more to help her return to work. Whatever the answer, one has to start by seeing the reality of what happens to women's lives after giving birth.

It's hard to believe women sit around over cups of tea saying, 'I had no idea a major life-changing event would affect my life.' But if they do, then all teenage girls should read *Shattered*, by Rebecca Asher, a book which details the profound disruption done to a woman's life by becoming a mother. Asher explains the exhaustion, loss of time, loss of identity, etc, after giving birth. Her former life is gone, and sometimes the career with it. While Asher bemoans the effects on women, she doesn't ignore the effects on men. As both parties are suffering under the current system, she believes there must be a better way.

It's a cause of grievance for some women that they end up doing more of the parenting and domestic work while the man continues his career. As a feminist would see it, women are excluded from the world of work and reduced to a lower status role as 'unpaid domestic servant.' They believe this is forced on them through systemic injustice - social expectations, government and employer policies, and presumably biology itself. While there's *some* truth to this view, there's a lot more to the story.

Is it unfair that a woman's career is harmed by having to take a year off for parenting? In some ways, but it's a complex issue. If parenting is seen as a chief cause of the pay gap, then the battle isn't just in the workplace but in the whole realm of marriage. Marriage itself becomes a battlefield over what you could call the three Rs - rights, roles, and responsibilities. The fight is about work, inside and outside the home. Who *gets* to do it (have a job or career), and who *has* to do it (the parenting and domestic work). Mind you, you could swap the bracketed comments in that sentence around.

In my view, apart from giving birth and the early period of parenting, there's no reason the work should be divided any particular way. There's no reason the father shouldn't take the parental leave and the mother keep her job. But there often *are* reasons why that doesn't happen, which may not be the man's fault.

Take the practice of hypergamy, which is women's tendency to 'marry up,' that is, to a higher status or wealthier man. This means after the baby is born, it is the man who 'has to' keep working simply because he earns more money for the family. Women might say this is unfair, to which one could reply, 'Stop practicing hypergamy. Marry a man with lower status and a lower paying job. Then it will be him who has to quit work and look after the baby while you carry on your career.'

Others complain it is Social Expectations which compel women to behave in a certain way. I'll capitalise the phrase to suggest the exaggerated power given to this hidden force. Most people are driven by the need for social approval and, on average, perhaps women feel it more than men. Yet ultimately, Social Expectations don't really force us to do anything, except to the degree we are cowed by them.

It's necessary to say this because the GPG debate often implies women have no agency and are just blown around like motes of dust by external forces. Perhaps the two main causes of the GPG are 1) women entering low paid professions and 2) women's careers being harmed when they become mothers. It does little good to say Social Expectations force women to do either of these things, unless your aim is to change those norms. To go down the path of low paid jobs and motherhood, blame it on Social Expectations, then spend the next decade using your husband as a punching bag for the patriarchy is a weak denial of personal responsibility.

If the battle in marriage is about work and how it's divided up, one must be proactive not reactive. First, anyone considering marriage and kids should read Rebecca Asher's *Shattered* to see if they still want to go down that path. If they do, there should be a frank discussion about who is going to do what in the marriage. If they can't reach an agreement on that, don't get married.

Obviously, most marriages don't develop that way. They begin in a romantic haze of blind optimism where it's assumed everyone will live happily ever after. Some couples spend more time planning the wedding than they do the marriage (and no, Social Expectations aren't making them do that either). Then, when things start to go south, the negotiation starts. This is all done on an *ad hoc* basis and the goalposts keep getting moved. By the time both parties hate each other, it's too late.

To repeat, apart from the early stages, there's no real reason it should be the woman who stays home and the man who keeps working. *Some* women, who don't like their jobs, are glad of a reason to give them up. No doubt there are some men who feel the same way about their jobs and would be happy to quit given the chance. In the present system, however, some women 'forced' to quit work after the baby feel deeply aggrieved and resent their husbands.

This is not really fair to the husbands. Some time ago, there was a series of articles by an American feminist I'll call Lara McGillivray, who had recently become a mother. One article in particular stood out. It began with a warm and fuzzy tone, then a couple of paragraphs in changed abruptly to a tone of bitterness and icy rebuke. Startled by the change, I backtracked and realised the first part was addressed to women, the author's sisters-in-suffering, while the rest was aimed at men. Lara wanted to make it clear just how difficult life was for new mothers, while admonishing men for their profound failings as human beings and their undeserved luck in not having to give birth.

In trying to glean what Lara's partner had done wrong, it seemed his main sin was the act of continuing to exist. To exist, that is, as anything but a selfless and devoted slave to the struggling mother and newborn. It was, for example, Grand Insolence on one occasion for the man to say that he wasn't feeling well, or some such remark. This made Lara fly into a rage. How, in vicinity to Lara's great martyrdom, did the husband dare complain about *anything*? On another night, he decided to go to the pub, a betrayal of such devastating selfishness it was grounds for divorce.

It seems that for Lara, her husband was now both a convenience and an inconvenience. He was useful for earning a wage and obeying her every command. Yet he had the audacity to still have wants of his own. This insubordination was sure to see him confined to the doghouse for some time to come, released only to go out and perform his duty as a wage slave.

Clearly, the first twelve months of parenthood are hard and the father has to play his fair part. Even so, there's no reason he should become his wife's personal punching bag. Reading between the lines of her articles, it was obvious Lara had become a living nightmare to be around. Even allowing for the difficult first year, Lara had gone above and beyond the call of duty and made it her personal mission to be as vindictive as possible on behalf of women as a class. Still, if motherhood was such a burden to her, you wonder why she agreed to it in the first place. A cynic might think her main reason for getting pregnant was to experience a new form of oppression.

While Lara is an extreme case, there are many lesser versions of the same thing. In a book called *How Not to Hate Your Husband After Kids*, Jancee Dunn mentions the tendency of new fathers to suddenly find reasons to be away from home. That is, the sudden development of new hobbies, pressing work business, and so on. While there's no doubt many fathers shirk their parenting, it's also likely some of them are married to versions of Lara. No wonder Lara's husband wanted to escape to the pub for a night. It's not that life isn't a struggle for new mothers - of course it's hard. But the ones that insist on becoming a living nightmare to punish men for their male privilege, the gender pay gap, or whatever other sins they haven't committed are also part of the problem.

There was a comment on one of Lara's articles by an older woman who'd been a mother in a previous generation, perhaps the 1970s. While she basically gave her approval, you could sense her bemusement at the idea of motherhood as one quarter Heaven and three quarters Hell. You could hear her thinking, 'Yes it was hard...but it wasn't *that* bad.' This couldn't possibly be to do with third-wave feminism's ever-evolving sense of women's agony, could it?

If the gender pay gap is one of the Five Pillars of Feminism, and motherhood one of its main causes, you might wonder why a feminist would go down that path and why male partners would want to go with them. We're not yet in the Republic of Gilead where women are forced to be mothers. Before taking that path, people need to know what they're in for. Women should ask their husbands, 'If we have children, are you going to give up a lot of your time and interests so you can support us financially and still do your share of the parenting?' In turn, men should ask their wives, 'If we have children, are you prepared to accept the life changes that will come? Or are you going to blame me for ruining your life, complain about the gender pay gap, and turn into Lara McGillivray?'

To repeat, much of the GPG struggle is about what happens in marriage around the three Rs - rights, roles, and responsibilities, in regard to work inside and outside the home. Who *gets* to do it (have a job or career), and who *has* to do it (the parenting and domestic work). In that case, it really has to be worked out ahead of time, rather than couples making policy on the run. Here are two ways women could approach marriage.

Option One (the current model): Get married in a state of blind optimism. Don't research the effects of having children. Don't think of how you want the marriage to work or communicate your wants and expectations. Fall into standard social norms of behaviour. Get pregnant and quit your job. After the baby is born, start to resent your husband when he has to keep working 'for financial reasons' while you do most of the domestic work. Suffer in silence for years while punishing him with a drip feed of passive aggression. After several years, explode in rage and leave him. Then complain about women's lot and how Social Expectations made all your life choices for you.

Option Two: If you're concerned women lose out financially in marriage, face the issue ahead of time. Realise the whole marriage and children package involves a lot of labour, both with paid work done outside the home to bring in wages, and 'unpaid' work in the home in parenting, housework, and so on. Decide how the entire pool of labour is going to be divided up between the wife and husband, being clear on what is desired and expected. If both parties can reach an agreement, get married. If they can't, don't.

Having said that, there's another slant on the story which is often overlooked. Feminist accounts of marriage usually say it's *women* who are blindsided by the demands of marriage, while the man benefits. This again ignores the real experiences of many men who find themselves drawn into a situation they didn't anticipate and may come to regret. A psychiatrist named Marty Nemko says that, on average, women are more motivated than men to have children while *expecting* the man to provide the higher wage that pays for it as well being ideal husbands and fathers. He speculates that if, before marriage, women told their husbands their real expectations of how the marriage will work, many men would bail out, 'so, most women withhold those demands until afterwards.' In other words, to say it is only women who are the 'victims' of marriage and children is to present a very one-sided view.

The Bigger Picture

Feminists usually see the GPG as a problem hurting women but not caused by them. Yet denying that individual choices play a part won't help. Even so, there are ways the overall system could be improved. Perhaps it *is* unfair women's careers are harmed by their desire to have children. Having children is not just a private act, but also benefits society at large, not least in its actual continuation. Those who take on that task should in some ways be supported. There still has to be personal responsibility and no one can 'have it all,' but there should also be an eye to the bigger picture.

The declining birth rates in Western nations have been noticed. Ironically, that has not been a problem in more patriarchal countries, only in the progressive West. Still, contrary to feminist belief, most Western men are not plotting some kind of *Handmaid's Tale* regime which puts women into bondage. Women have the same right as men to pursue careers. If motherhood is damaging their career prospects to the extent that they're deterred from having children, the government and employers should take some steps to make it easier for them.

What form this takes is for others to work out, but you'd imagine it would require practical steps (e.g. paid parental leave for men) and a change of attitude (men and women are both responsible for the early years of parenting). Parental leave systems vary from country to country. It's said that Sweden has a good paternal leave system (well, at least until the Caliphate comes into power) whereas Germany, for a fair while, did not - largely ruling out motherhood for high level career women. No wonder they had a declining birth rate.

Employers should also play *some* part, although this isn't easy. In *Shattered*, Rebecca Asher notes that many UK companies want employees who make work their top priority. They tend to have little patience for the needs of parents. In the competitive world of business, companies' main concern is the bottom line, and a wider regard for the social good will lag far behind. Overcoming that won't be easy.

You can't really expect companies to deviate too far from their main purpose, which presumably is to make a profit. Asher says all UK employees should have an automatic right to flexible working hours, and should not have to wait six months to receive it. That may be going too far. Companies exist to do business, not just as convenient supports to parents. The need to compete makes certain demands on them. Getting a balance between profit and a wider social concern isn't an easy problem to solve.

Some feminists think such companies are driven by 'male values' like competitiveness and aggression. If so, it's time for an experiment in which companies run and staffed only by women are set up. Such companies could have full control over their internal policies. They could grant as much parental leave and flexible hours as they liked, with the added benefits of not having to complain about sexism, harassment, or the GPG. Maybe these companies would succeed and serve as a model for others. However, they might find the sting of economic competition gave them more empathy for how their previous companies were run. It could be that capitalism, after all, has little to do with gender and is just mathematics. It's easier, say, to support granting maternal leave for a recent employee as a bystander rather than when you're the boss who actually has to pay it.

It is here, perhaps, where the government might step in and pay for the parental leave, rather than leaving it up to the company. Overall, it is a difficult balance. There's a need for a big picture approach to supporting parents who are, after all, helping our species to continue. To what degree it is the responsibility of government, employers, or individuals is too big a question for me to take on here.

The Illusion of Privilege

While the system should take steps to make it easier for mothers, we should also have sympathy for men and dispense with the idea their lives are nothing but ease and glory. In terms of the GPG, feminists tell a tale of the woman whose career is cruelly sabotaged by long periods off work to raise children. Meanwhile, her husband's male privilege lets him continue his ascent to the top of the corporate world. While that's true in some cases, it's a very partial view of the situation which rests on the recurring false premise that life is always easier for men.

The idea that being the only wage earner for a family is a

privilege is a false assumption to begin with. If we rounded up a thousand single parents, they'd set us straight about how fine a blessing it is to grind out a living as the sole breadwinner. There was a recent article about women who found themselves earning all the family's money when their partners were out of action for whatever reason. Turns out they didn't much like it, so being the sole wage earner may not be such a privilege after all. Who'd have thought?

Who, after all, is the man doing this for? Contrary to what one may hear, it is not solely for his own greater glory, but for his partner and children. Once again, there's no reason the woman *shouldn't* take on this role. Many men might let them have it. But it should come with a government warning that the privilege of being sole wage earner isn't all it's cracked up to be.

It's not as if the man necessarily loves his work. If we're going to talk about the tyranny of Social Expectations, it's worth looking at the sort of jobs men are socialised into. While some women are studying STEM these days, they still far out-number men in *relatively* low paid jobs like teaching or nursing. While these are noble professions, money can't be the main motivation for those who choose them. Presumably they think these jobs will suit them, or they'll like the work.

As Warren Farrell has said, choosing a career because they like the work is an example of female privilege. Many women who become nurses or teachers also want to own a home and have a family, neither of which is possible on a nurse or teacher's salary (at least in a city like Sydney, where I live). How then are they expecting the dream of home and family to come true? Take a guess.

A man is also aware of Social Expectations, one of which is that if he wants to own a home and have a family, he'll need a high paying job to achieve it. He'll also be vaguely aware of hypergamy, and that women will expect him to be a good financial provider to enable that house and family. Under those pressures, he does not have the privilege of choosing a vocational career based on liking the work.

It may also be that in having the house and family, a man is responding to his partner's desire more than his own. Marty Nemko, who has done a lot of career counselling, tells a story about a real life couple, 'Kevin' and 'Lisa.' This isn't the sort of story you'll find on a government website, and certainly not one aimed at 'fixing the gender pay gap.' Yet it's surely as common as the story of William and Amelia given earlier.

> Kevin, 37, is a computer programmer, making $80,000 a year, $48,000 after taxes. His wife, Lisa, stays home to take care of their two-year old. She is pregnant with another child, and eager for them to buy a home. Kevin doesn't like being a programmer, but fears that a career change will mean a salary cut.

> I asked Kevin, "Is owning a home important to you?" He replied, "It's very important to Lisa." I asked him how he felt about having the second child. He sighed, "Okay, but Lisa really wants it."

> I asked, "When you first called me, you said you feel the stress is killing you. Should you be shouldering all the family's financial responsibilities?" He pursed his lips: "Lisa reminds me that before we got married, I agreed to have two kids. She says, and I guess I agree, that to bring our kids up right and maintain a home is a full-time job. And she insists she has no earning capacity. Not true. She certainly could get a restaurant server job, which pays well. And I'm reading that kids turn out at least as well if they have a working mom."

Mind you, Lisa doesn't have to work in a restaurant. She could pursue any number of part time jobs. She could also train for a full time job, which might allow Kevin to stay home as the main parent. If, in the past, she had trained as an IT worker, it might have been her earning the $80,000 income as an IT worker instead of her husband.

A different article on the GPG says women are the main victims after giving birth because their employment hours drastically decrease, while the husband's hours may not change at all. However this may not be male privilege, as the article implies, but the urgent need to make a living for the family. Rebecca Asher concedes that while some men expect their wives to be the main parent, plenty of women expect their husbands to be the wage earner. In some cases, he may be accommodating his wife's wishes more than his own, if he has been pressured into parenthood in the first place.

It's true that some mothers would prefer to resume their careers rather than taking on the burden of parenthood and domestic labour. In other words, they would swap places with their husbands - and should have the option to do so. But it's dishonest to suggest that all, or even most, mothers think like this. How many would really want to take on the burden of being the sole or main wage earner? For various reasons, some women prefer their husbands take the role. Nemko again, says:

> Most of my male clients have accepted their plight of having to work, work, work at unrewarding, even dangerous jobs. Biology, parents, and society have programmed men to be the hunter, the provider, to keep their nose to the grindstone, no matter what. Too many wives only encourage it. Just today, a client of mine who earns more than $200,000 a year as a not-partner attorney at a major law firm, exclaimed, "If I

don't push NOW to make partner, my wife will kill me!"

Usually, the wife won't kill the husband, but often will divorce him, at least in part because "he wasn't a good provider." And most courts reward her with custody of the child and a requirement that the father pay child support and / or alimony.

When I ask a male client to step back and think about it, many of them realize that their wives have tried - usually successfully - to subtly or not so subtly coerce them into being the primary or sole breadwinner, the beast of burden.

Being the main wage earner isn't a privilege. It's not as if everyone loves their job. Would giving women this 'privilege' make them happier? Perhaps not. Once again, there is a certain amount of work involved in a marriage, some outside the home and some inside. In the end - or preferably, in the beginning - it is really up to each couple to stop pretending Social Expectations are dictating terms and negotiate how this work is going to be divided up.

Take housework, for example. If both parents are working fulltime (say, by the time the children are in school), it is fair to divide the housework equally between them. Yet if the wife is working full time and the husband only part time, she's probably not going to want to do half of the housework when she gets home. In the feminist-friendly media, we always hear about the hard lot of the working mother, but Asher notes that men are hardly much better off. Many of them are answering to a demanding boss or clients during the day, then coming home exhausted and asked to be the perfect husband and father as well.

In this chapter, I've tried to suggest that the gender pay gap is largely an argument about the roles, rights, and responsibilities within marriage, and that the pay gap, if it's a problem at all, is partly caused by women's choices - which aren't the fault of Social Expectations but women's acquiescence to them. I've also suggested that male privilege isn't all it's cracked up to be, and that it's possible for women to beat the GPG if they address two of its main causes: choosing lower paid professions, and the question of marriage and how it affects them.

Even so, there's a bigger impediment to be overcome. It's little to do with external reality and more about a state of mind which insists that, no matter what happens, women will always be victims of the GPG and general injustice. It's a state of mind you might call toxic martyrdom.

11
Complaining is Not a Strategy

Toxic Martyrdom

Suppose someone made a strong case that the pay gap isn't an injustice against women. The problem - if it's even a problem at all - is easily fixed by *individual* women doing some things and avoiding others. And whatever else it is caused by, men are mostly not to blame.

The reasonable response would be one of relief. What a relief to move on from the idea that you're permanently ripped off. But most feminists wouldn't do that. They'd go on believing the GPG is a crime against women. To persist in this belief is a case of what I will call toxic martyrdom, a state of mind where one refuses to give up a belief in persecution.

A martyr is 'someone who suffers persecution and death for advocating, renouncing, refusing to renounce, or refusing to advocate a belief or cause as demanded by an external party.' Of course, the belief might be in something that is worthy, or at least true. A toxic martyr, however, is someone who clings to a belief that is false because the attachment to persecution is so strong.

There are other mental problems related to this. One is being so focused on a given problem that it distorts your perception of the world. So, GPG activists may be so obsessed with money they forget people's choices are based on many factors, not just maximising income.

Another is the tendency to blame all one's problems on external forces. Most situations arise from a mix of internal factors within a person's control and external factors outside their control. Believing all problems are externally caused shows an unhealthy state of mind. The current chapter will look at this in terms of the GPG.

The Denial of Choice

As mentioned, two of the main reasons for the GPG are that women tend to choose lower paid professions, and do more of the parenting and domestic work. There's no real reason they *have* to do either of these things. Yet enough women are continuing to do them that the GPG remains. While some girls are now studying the higher paid STEM fields (science, technology, engineering, and math), many still choose the lower paid careers. Young women continue to have families even though it harms their earnings. Still, these trends are mystifying only if you look at everything in terms of money. Perhaps when all's said and done, most people have higher priorities than doing their bit to end the gender pay gap.

At this point, GPG activists could throw up their hands and say, 'We warned them. If they don't listen, that's their problem.' Instead, they hold to the unshakeable belief that the GPG proves the terrible plight of women and *something must be done* about it. The usual tack is to say women aren't really choosing low paid jobs and parenting, Social Expectations are making them do it.

This strategy isn't all bad. Pointing out that Social Expectations shouldn't dictate people's behaviour is a first step, which should be followed by the second step of telling women that they don't *have* to do most of the parenting any more than they *have* to train for the lower paid professions.

Where the strategy falls down is that 'Social Expectations' becomes an excuse. It also means seeing women as a class rather than individuals. It's not as if one particular woman's life choices are forcing another to do the same. Why should a female high flyer even care about the GPG? She would know the pay gap is based on the average wage of all women working full time. That figure of 80c isn't based on *her* salary, but on the many women working in lower paid professions. CEOs don't get to the top by caving to peer approval, and the female exec would know it was precisely in rejecting Social Expectations that she'd been able to reach her current level.

For the many other women earning less, one would think they never had any part in their life choices. It was Social Expectations that made the choices for them. Karen Straughan, a critic of feminism, has a theory of 'agents and objects.' She says a feminist worldview implies that men are agents who act, and women are objects who are acted upon.

This entails the disempowering view that women have little part in causing the events of their lives. Remember this isn't women under the Taliban or in the fictional Handmaid Republic, but in Western nations. For an activist movement like feminism, there's a strange sense of passivity in the idea that reforms don't have to come from the behaviour of individual women, but from external sources - men, the system, or the government. Equality is something not to be seized but legislated. We live in an 'excuse culture' with the perennial cry of *something should be done* ! In the context of a much longer talk, Karen Straughan says:

> In other words, women don't make choices. Choices are made for women by society, by institutions, by circumstances, and by men. Women need not adapt their choices, actions, behaviours, and priorities in order to become empowered through their own actions. Society, institutions, circumstances, and men should all adapt so that women - inert objects that they are perceived to be - can have an obstacle-free path along which they will be guided by encouragement,

steered in the proper directions and not forced to change course by any difficulty, real or imaginary, so that empowerment can be gotten for them...

Agents make things happen, and objects have things happen to them. In the gendered worldview of feminism and the wider culture, women cannot be counted on to make things happen, they must have things be made to happen for them. They're objects, not agents.

Imagine a girl named Sal who enrols in university to do an Arts degree. Or rather, imagine a 'sliding doors' scenario where there are two Sals - Sal A and Sal B. In her first year, Sal takes an introductory gender studies subject and learns about the pay gap. Sal A realises an Arts degree is less likely to lead to a high paid profession and changes course for her second year to something more lucrative like engineering or IT. In an alternate world, Sal B stays with the Arts degree and spends the next twenty years complaining about the pay gap without taking any steps to remedy it apart from complaining - and complaining is not a strategy.

At this point we should recall the flawed premise in the whole debate, which is the idea that money is all that counts. *People do not make their life choices based on money alone.* Why should Sal give up her Arts degree just because engineering or IT leads to a higher salary? Yet within the flawed terms of the debate, if Sal is genuinely worried about the GPG, the empowering thing to do is change her course.

Suppose that five years later Sal's started work, but she's thinking about marrying a man and having children. Sal knows about the GPG and that parenthood will harm her career. So, Sal A could tell her partner very clearly in advance that if they marry, she won't be taking on the bulk of the childcare and domestic work. Alternately, Sal B could just move in without any discussion, get pregnant and take a year off work, then complain that Social Expectations ruined her life.

In terms of Karen Straughan's theory, Sal A is an agent, and Sal B is an object. In speaking about Social Expectations, perhaps feminists are trying to help women move from B to A, but it often feels like they're saying women are stuck at B and it's up to men, the government, or the system to guide them to A without the women having to take any responsibility for doing it themselves.

We seem to live in an Excuse Culture where there's always something stopping women getting ahead - and it's always something *external*. As an example of this sort of thinking, a 2018 newspaper article called 'Acting Wife' listed three problems faced by women in the corporate world.

The first was only mentioned in passing - that many women feel burdened by the need to run a household and manage its occupants' needs. The second was their added burden of mastering the corporate dress code. While men only need an expensive suit, some white shirts, and a few ties, women have to decide between pants or skirt, get the right colours, choose the appropriate amount of jewellery and makeup, and decide on shoes, pantihose, and hair style. This is yet more evidence of male privilege.

To begin, we might question the idea that women's careers are harmed because they're forced to run a household and serve its members. How are Social Expectations making them do this? Are Social Expectations forcing women to have children, run a perfect household, do the bulk of the domestic work, or even have relationships in the first place? Despite what anyone says, no one is really making women do any of these things. While the need for social approval runs deep in human nature,

Social Expectations only control you if you give in to them.

If such a woman thinks running a household will kill her career, she should tell her partner upfront she's not prepared to do it. If he's not happy, don't marry him. Marry someone else, stay single, or work out another way to run the household. Don't give in to Social Expectations like you have no choice, then spend the next ten years complaining.

As for the clothes and makeup, of course women's attire is more complicated than men's. While this must be annoying, at the end of the day, board members are going to judge a woman on the quality of her work, not on whether she's wearing the right shoes-jewellery-scarf combination. A tough minded woman shouldn't be cowed by what other people think, and if need be, she should buy five simple outfits and rotate them. You know, like the men do. If the woman is doing a brilliant job, no one will care what she's wearing.

Some will angrily reply by saying, *you've got no idea how harshly women are judged...by other women*. Sure, but if they care so much what others think, that's part of the problem. Committing the *faux pas* of wearing last month's fashions isn't something CEOs of either gender should give a damn about.

The article then goes on to its main point, which is that behavioural traits that are thought to enhance women's relationship prospects harm their careers. Apparently, in the dating world, women are sometimes told to downplay their talents, brains, ambition, etc, so as to make themselves appealing to men, who supposedly find those traits intimidating. Such women are 'acting wife' to attract men.

The article cites studies claiming the same traits are filtering through to the workplace, where they harm the women's careers. It seems that young female workers are reining themselves in if male colleagues are around. According to the author, even some of the best and brightest young women are doing this.

There are a few problems with this argument. First, what does romance have to do with the workplace? People shouldn't be thinking about relationships when they go to work. Even if some types of behaviour are good for attracting mates, there's no reason to display them in the office, which calls for a different mindset. Second, why would strong, intelligent women be interested in the type of men who find them intimidating? Third, if their main concern is being attractive to arrogant young businessmen, they don't sound like CEO material in the first place.

Yet the main problem is the idea that women have no agency of their own and are forced to behave a certain way by other people's expectations. It's implied that they absorb behavioural norms by osmosis. Once again, they are 'objects' who simply *react* to external influences, in a way that harms their careers. And the conclusion? *Something should be done* - by other people or by society at large - to stop women's behaviour being controlled.

This sort of thing identified in this article is useful up to a point - in showing women they need not accept external cues on how to behave. Beyond that - the idea that women are reactive objects and other people should *stop making them do things* - should be rejected too. Again, the compulsion to please others is not the stuff of which CEOs are made. If women want to be CEOs, this sort of weak, reactive behaviour should be viewed with more scorn than sympathy, and should be purged as unworthy of her career ambitions.

Yes, Social Expectations do influence our actions. Recognising that is a useful first step. But giving in to them then complaining is rather pathetic. How many CEOs have complained their way to the top? Complaining is not a strategy.

A Detour Onto the Highway to Hell

In writing about the gender pay gap, I don't speak as one of life's winners. It's not a case of *I made it to the top, so anyone can*; but rather *I'm down here like you - so what?* The theory of male privilege implies that the mere possession of a penis (and preferably a white one) guarantees a rails ride to the top of any profession. It's a lie. Getting to the top is hard - *for everyone*. Feminists need to stop translating a universal problem into a gendered one.

At the risk of shocking my readers, I'm not a CEO or a millionaire, and don't possess any of the worldly success that would make me the envy of pay gap activists. Should I complain about how *it ain't fair*? I *could*, and at times I certainly *have*, but that state of mind is a poor route to happiness. At no point will I try to argue that the world is fair. My point is it's unfair to everyone, not just women or other 'victim groups.'

See, I did an Arts degree too. It wasn't very lucrative financially, but it enriched my life in other, more important ways. I also spent plenty of years in music. In terms of businesses that are unfair and poorly paid, the music biz is certainly one you could file under Industries That Suck. Only a handful of musicians make any real money out of it, though plenty spend their best years trying.

An example of 'male privilege' given earlier was that most of the Triple J Hottest 100 Songs are by men. Rest assured that the music biz sucks for both men and women. If more men than women do it, it's probably because they're willing to endure the relentless, grinding, uncomfortable lifestyle that is required to make it in rock music. Supposedly a glamour life, the reality is late nights, poor sleep, discomfort, and years slogging it out for meagre reward - and that was in the good old days! It's much worse now.

When AC/DC's Bon Scott sang *It's a Long Way to the Top*,

did he benefit from male privilege in finally getting there? Maybe - in the sense that his mental and physical toughness helped him endure the grinding rock touring life he called the *Highway to Hell*. But by the time he drank himself to death at the age of thirty-three, he had only a few bucks in the bank. Male privilege? Er...maybe not.

There were some tough female rockers around at the time - women like Suzi Quatro or Chrissie Amphlett - but, on average, women are less willing to put up with the sheer physical hardship that goes with that sort of life. In saying this, I'm not berating women so much as putting myself in the same category, because I wouldn't want to endure it either. Yet it's almost a requirement if you want to make it in rock music. It's not fair, but that's the way it is.

Who Wants to Be a CEO?

Yet there's one job which is apparently more coveted than any other - that of being a CEO. It always comes up in pay gap discussions - although it's not clear why a tiny elite group should be the gold standard for measuring gender equality overall. Superficially, a CEO job does look like a glittering prize - as long as you ignore the disadvantages, such as the need to be a workaholic and rarely see your family. Why aren't there more female CEOs? If half of the population are women, why aren't half the number of CEOs women? Maybe because they want to have a life.

Speaking for myself, I often wake up in the morning and wonder why I'm not a CEO. Then I remember I took an Arts degree at uni, like to have a personal life and leisure time, and don't want to do sixty hour work weeks or be on call 24-7. There are plenty of women who aren't CEOs for similar reasons.

But what about the ones trained in business who do want

to go to the top? They have a chance if they take the same route as the men who want those positions, especially if they remain childfree. Those who want children face another hurdle. Unfair? Probably, considering most male CEOs have non-working wives who can parent their children full time. Women who want to be CEOs and have children need to find a partner who'll take on that role. This trend has yet to catch on. Hypergamy - women marrying men with higher wealth and status - plays a part in this. The trait is far less common in men. Male CEOs have few qualms about marrying women with less money and status. Unless female execs are prepared to do it too, those who want a family will struggle to make CEO level.

Some feminists are trying to change the culture of the business world. In her book *Stop Fixing Women*, Catherine Fox discusses this in great detail. She claims to have seen changes of attitude from corporate men. Her mission is to get a better deal for women in that environment. If she can pull it off, so be it. Those sympathetic to her agenda will find her book worth reading. Others will be harder to convince.

One push to make workplaces more female-friendly is to bring in flexible hours and part time positions. However, while that would benefit mid-level workers, it may not help those at the top. Few of the top positions in the corporate world are filled by those working part time, or even those working forty hour weeks. In an article called 'The Real Reason So Few Women Are in the Boardroom,' Marty Nemko says:

> If I were a CEO, I would certainly want to hire women in senior positions, but only those with a proven track record of having put in long hours at work and in professional development, and who could be counted on to continue doing so. Those are the same criteria I would use to evaluate male candidates.

Women, if you want to be considered for the boardroom, it doesn't cut it to say you're working smart so you needn't work long hours. There are plenty of men competing for those slots who work both long and smart. You can't have it both ways: either plan on working long and smart or accept a lower-level job in exchange for work / life balance.

There would be plenty of room in my company for women and men who want to work a moderate workweek, but not at the top. I don't care whether my executives have a Y chromosome, but I want their priority not to be work / life balance, but rather, helping my company to ethically develop the best products in the world.

This may seem unfair to women, but it's actually unfair to *anyone* who wants work / life balance. Reaching the top in most professions demands sacrifices of the things most people take for granted. That's part of the 'privilege' of being a CEO, people who are in some respects to be pitied, not envied. These sort of sacrifices are often dictated not by men, but by the industry itself, which is highly competitive due to pressures both internal and external. Internal, in that the job of CEO is coveted by other ambitious people, and external in the need to compete with business rivals in the capitalist system.

Regardless of this, there are currently some strong efforts to get more women into CEO jobs. There are several reasons this won't be easy, one of which is that ambitious, competitive men are unlikely to just step aside. One high placed female exec thinks a reason men aren't supportive is because now they're competing with 100% of the population rather than 50%. The problem with statements like that is men will say, *You want to compete? Let's compete.* Should men make it easier for women? Given that feminism has been so adversarial, it's hard to see why men would adopt some kind of 'he-for-she' stance. In the end, it may not be men who dictate terms but the work itself. Here's Nemko again:

> Imagine you were the CEO of a company and were considering two employees for a senior position. Candidate A had - over her or his 20-year career - worked 50 to 60 hours a week, and in spare time, made great efforts to keep upgrading skills. Meanwhile, Candidate B worked 40 hours a week, and in spare time, focused on family, home, friends, and recreation, and had taken years off to raise children - thereby losing professional contacts and currency with the latest information and technology. You'd almost certainly hire Candidate A. Fact is, more men than women are like Candidate A. That, and not a sexist glass ceiling, is the main reason why women represent only 11% of senior executives in Fortune 500 companies.
>
> But let's say that you, the CEO, did what feminist activists advocate: install a family-friendly workplace that prioritizes work-life balance, and hired many women who had worked only 40 hours a week and taken years off to raise children. You might hire lots of people like Candidate B. If so, your company would likely go out of business.

The lack of female CEOs is supposed to prove the injustice of the gender pay gap. Yet there are long causal processes that lead to people becoming CEOs. Pay gap activists want to argue these processes discriminate against women. That's a matter of opinion. Another question to consider might be, why would you want to be a CEO in the first place? And why is the gender makeup of an elite profession making up 0.01% of the population, to be used as a measure of general social equality? Commonsense aside, it's likely the lack of female CEOs will remain a key argument for the gender pay gap, and will help stir up a misplaced sense of grievance in women for some time to come.

12

From the GPG to the KAM

Did you know that women 'work for free' from November to January and they're cheated of $13,000 a year in wages? These claims appeared in a Sydney newspaper in 2017. If true, women should be angry. Just one problem - it's complete bullshit, based on a false interpretation of the gender pay gap stats. That doesn't stop this lie being used as a reason to resent men as a class. It's a short and winding road from the GPG to the KAM. That is, from the Gender Pay Gap to the Kill All Men, which was a popular slogan on Twitter a while back.

Silly ideas can have silly consequences. If you asked a computer the best way to fix the GPG, its answer would be both logical and obtuse. Women should: 1. study finance, IT, or engineering; 2. work at least fifty hours a week in their jobs and 3. never marry or have children. It would also say women as a class should do this, not just those who want to.

While some women would agree, most wouldn't. Why should they? People should be allowed to seek fulfilling jobs, work-life balance, and parenthood - even if all these lead to the wage gap.

But suppose that computer somehow took over the world and put its GPG reforms into action. The unintended consequences would be many women having to do jobs they don't like, working long hours, and not having families or leisure time. Strange as it seems, that might not make them happy.

Some jobs are higher paid for a reason. Jim Goad's article, 'Smashing Through the Glass Coffin,' noted that few women are trying to break into high paid but dangerous professions like logging and fishing. There's a reason 90% of workplace deaths are men. Pay gap ascendency comes with a price.

Apparently there's even a pay gap between male and female Uber drivers, and the main reasons are that men drive faster and take jobs at more dangerous times and places. So that's an easy fix. All women Uber drivers have to do is drive faster and take more dangerous jobs.

Some jobs are lower paid for a reason. Warren Farrell believes 'many of the low-paid jobs are low-paid because they are safer, have higher fulfilment, more flexible hours, and other desirable traits that make them more in demand and thus lower in pay. When *either* sex chooses jobs with these traits, they can expect low pay.' Farrell identifies eight factors which contribute to being lower paid.

1. The ability to psychologically 'check out' at the end of the day.
2. Physical safety.
3. Indoors.
4. Low risk.
5. Desirable or flexible hours.
6. No demands to move out of town.
7. High fulfilment relative to training.
8. Contact with people in a pleasant environment.

Several of these are associated with the so called 'female professions.' All of them play a part in causing the dreaded pay gap.

Let's make a final visit to the business world and imagine there were 100 candidates for 10 CEO jobs. Suppose being a CEO required a person to have been a workaholic for years and given up family and work-life balance.

Let's say that out of the top 10 who had done that, 8 were men and 2 were women. If you're like Canadian PM, Justin Trudeau, you'll say 'Because it's 2019!' and give out the jobs to 5 men and 5 women. This is equality with a crowbar - and if you think it's fair, rewrite the paragraph like this:

Let's say that out of the top 10 who had done that, 8 were women and 2 were men. If you're like Canadian PM, Justin Trudeau, you'll say 'Because it's 2019!' and give out the jobs to 5 men and 5 women.

Still think it's fair?

We need to tell people ahead of time what it takes to get the job, then give them equal chance to compete. Justice is about equality of opportunity, not equality of outcome.

Apart from that, when it comes to doing a CEO job, what has a person's gender got to do with it in the first place? If we accept the premise that both sexes are equally capable, we should be ignoring gender, not fixating on it.

No one is saying the world of work is fair or ruled by merit alone. The 'Matthew Effect' applies in most fields. That is, that those who already have power tend to get more opportunities and reward than those without power, so it's a recurring cycle. Women suffer from the Matthew Effect, but so do men. Thomas Malthus wrote in the eighteenth century that we are all 'born into a world already possessed.'

Men too are born powerless. Yet the GPG myth is an ongoing cause of anger against them. 'Kill All Men' was a popular Twitter hash tag for a while. It was a joke, of course, and a very hilarious one. Still the GPG is certainly one path to the KAM, with its basis in envy and resentment.

Why are women left behind after motherhood while men race to the summit of their professions? While their husbands' careers advance, new mothers are left at home minding the baby. These ideas from Jane Asher's *Shattered* show the way some women feel, while forgetting for a moment that most men aren't anywhere near that fabled 'summit.' Many are plodding along in tedious jobs, wage slaves in the service of children and mortgages. Elsewhere in her book, Asher notes that plenty of men are also frustrated by their lot.

Feminism has always been an oppositional movement, defining itself as a struggle against men. The famous 2018 interview between Cathy Newman and Jordan Peterson is a good example of this state of mind. Newman is convinced the GPG is unfair but she doesn't seem to understand what causes it. She also tries her best to portray Peterson as sexist or misogynist and fails each time. This sort of misplaced anger was state of the art feminism in 2018.

At one point, Newman accused Peterson of being divisive, of 'riling people up.' Anti-feminist Karen Straughan made a commentary on this, saying:

> If the pay gap is (no one's fault)...then there'd be nothing for women to be angry about. There'd be no reason for women to resent men. Or feel stirred up, and resentful, and vindictive. Or see men as having taken things away from them. Leading people to believe they're being treated unfairly when they're not is the definition of 'riling them up'...

> And what is feminism, other than a division between men and women? What is it other than a philosophy that declares the interest of men and women to not only be fundamentally separate from one another, but also in conflict and competition. Feminism pits men and women against each other regarding wages. Regarding sex, regarding housework, regarding childcare, regarding [adopts tone of deep sarcasm] *emotional labour*, regarding air conditioning for crying out loud. Remember Cathy when Peterson talked about encouraging men, you were the one who asked 'what's in it for women?'

Is the GPG really a problem? Basically, people want to be happy and there's far more to that than having a big salary. In the many paths taken in pursuit of happiness, one hugely overrated side effect is that the average wage of all women working fulltime is less than the average wage of all men working fulltime.

And so what?

Of course, there can be improvements. Some jobs *are* undervalued. Maybe some of the so called 'female professions' should be paid more. School teaching, for one, given how hard the job is and the importance of the role. With the extra demands of the profession these days, some school teachers are working a lot more hours than they are paid for.

In the same way, there might be steps to help mothers return to the workforce, and fathers should have the option to be the main parent. Girls can study IT and engineering if that's what they want. Women can try to become CEOs as long as they're willing to compete with other people chasing the same goal.

These are reasonable ways in which the pay gap could be improved. Other ways are less reasonable. One academic complained that girls are more educated than ever before and this should be reflected in wages - but educated in what? Some universities teach activism these days, rather than employable skills. You can't choose to study a course that leads to a low paying career, or to no career at all, and then complain about the pay gap. In the same way, you can't choose a job that is safe, comfortable, and fulfilling and expect to be one of the top earners.

However, the simplest way to solve the problem of the GPG is to realise it's based on the false premise that money leads to happiness. You can also realise statistics about a class of people need not affect an individual member of that class, and that the privilege of being a high wage earner may be an illusion.

In hindsight, we may come to view the GPG as the sort

of 'problem' that arises when we take the concept of equality to the point of parody. We start with the premise that equality is a worthy ideal, then take it to the ridiculous conclusion that the income of all men and all women working fulltime has to average out exactly the same.

Of course, I may be wrong, and others will try to refute my arguments. But even if I'm right, some people will be unconvinced by anything I have said. The belief in persecution is too strong. Some others may know the GPG isn't a crime against women, but cynically go along with the lie to get sympathy and legal reforms in their favour.

Let's hope we can soon move on from the GPG and its false sense of grievance. Those prepared to lay the burden down may be surprised by the relief it brings. On the other hand, those who cling to persecution at any cost should move to Fecunda - as will be explained in the second last chapter of this book.

13

The Vast and the Spurious

Feminism was right about some things. Imagine being a woman before 1960. You were assumed to be less able and intelligent. You were given less education, shut out from positions of power, and largely confined to the domestic sphere. You were thought to be secondary to a man and dependent on one. You were expected to behave in certain ways and not others.

Most men would not like to be born into those conditions where the possibility of what they could do and be was so restricted.

At the same time, it's silly to think women enjoyed no benefits, or were all unhappy. Some feminists paint marriage in those days as a form of slavery, with women as unpaid domestic servants to their lordly husbands. I used to believe them, until hearing a couple of anti-feminists point out that this is way too simplistic. Karen Straughan said that plenty of men, especially in the harder jobs, were also slaves - just of a different type. Can anyone see the life of a coal miner as one of privilege? Another critic, Paul Elam, said he couldn't think of many slaves whose fairytale wish was to be chosen by a slave owner, nor were there many slave holders who got down on one knee to beg for ownership of the slave they wanted.

While life for plenty of housewives was a dull cycle of domestic labour (see Angela Holdsworth's book *Out of the Doll's House*, for example), the slavery analogy doesn't stand up to scrutiny. It may be truer to see pre-1960s marriage as a contract with a strict division of labour, one party working in the home, the other outside. As Straughan also said, the domestic labour was hardly 'unpaid.' The social contract was that the man was expected to hand over a portion of his wage as part of the deal.

It was his duty to support his wife and children.

As many feminists have said, strict gender roles can be stifling. A key reason for feminism was to overthrow the limits on potential for those who happen to be born female. To repeat, most men would not like to have been so constrained. For the record, I support the right of any individuals to try to do or be whatever they want.

So why write a book criticising feminism? Because while the main point of the movement - to free women from stifling gender roles - was a just cause, you've got to wonder where all the other rubbish has come from, and why there is more hatred between men and women today than ever before. Feminism, for all its origins as a liberation movement, has played a part in that.

As mentioned, plenty of feminists will be affronted that a man would dare discuss their favourite topic, which they think only women are allowed to talk about. But the reason men should discuss it is obvious - because they are routinely blamed for women's problems, or seen as having unearned privileges. Despite feminist denials that they hate men, there's no doubt their beliefs lead to antagonism towards men - and as many of those beliefs are false, this leads to a fair amount of return antagonism towards women.

Feminists expect to be able to rain down blow after blow upon men, and do so with impunity. Well, not any more - that's not how equality works. This book is a return of fire, but it's not meant to be too one-sided. The aim is to accept feminism's legitimate grievances, yet argue against those which are false.

Feminism is the vast and the spurious because it is a gigantic beast made of many ideas of variable worth. While some of these ideas are fair, others are distorted, out of date, or just plain wrong. This book offers my views on which are which. Naturally, some of my opinions will be wrong, and some people will disagree. Yet others will agree, and that might play a small part in stopping feminism becoming even more cult-like and divisive than it is today - and perhaps there will be less hatred between men and women.

To begin, it's worth revisiting what I called the Five Pillars of Feminism.

The Five Pillars of Feminism

1. Male Privilege - that men are automatically better off than women in most areas of life.
2. Patriarchal Control - that women live under social structures that favour men. Women's behaviour is limited by various rules and expectations.
3. Sexism - that women are seen as lesser beings, talked down to, and otherwise not given the same respect as men.
4. Sexual Assault and Harassment - that women face a constant battle against the threat of sexual violence and unwanted attention.
5. The Gender Pay Gap - that women are paid less, discriminated against in the workplace, and forced to do more unpaid domestic labour, which harms their financial power.

Taking these five pillars in reverse order: pillar five, the gender pay gap, has already been discussed. Pillar four about rape and harassment is obviously a reality women have to contend with.

I also accept the basic premise of pillar three, that people should not be treated as lesser beings on the basis of their gender. Yet neither should they get special favours. They should be treated on their individual merits.

Pillar two - the idea that women live in a male-dominated

world of patriarchal control - may be true if we're talking about a) non-Western countries, b) the Western world before 1970, or c) the fictional Republic of Gilead in *The Handmaid's Tale*. The idea that women in Western nations *today* are systematically oppressed is a myth.

That leaves pillar one - male privilege. The notion that men are better off than women in almost all areas of life is feminism's central idea. Notice that the emotions that go with this are envy and resentment. Yet this idea is also largely a myth. Men are better off in some areas of life and women are better off in others. Feminists have focussed on male advantages to such an extent that it's all they see. Still, some of their grievances are legitimate and these won't be ignored.

When I began writing this book, it was in the form of two long essays, originally called 'Agony: Much Worse Than Yours,' and 'The Vast and the Spurious.' The first was mainly about issues of work, money, etc, but did not give enough time to the idea of male privilege in social behaviour. The second essay was meant to address this.

Feminists are right that women have had to put up with a lot of annoying behaviour, some of which will come up in the next chapter, 'Dickheads Anonymous.' But while some grievances about male privilege are legit, others are just whining or bordering on a persecution complex. It's a matter of opinion which are which - and I'll certainly be giving mine.

My main source for the next few chapters is an article called '160+ Examples of Male Privilege in All Areas of Life' that was published on the *Everyday Feminism* website in 2016. That's recent enough to be a fair gauge of current thought.

Criticism of this list is not aimed at its author, so much as the belief system she is trying honestly to represent. Therefore, I won't refer to the author, but will speak only of the list itself. Where referring to a specific example, I'll mention 'item 73' or 'point 96' and so on out of those 167 points.

The male privilege list deals with nine main areas: 1. social norms, 2. sex and relationships, 3. harassment and violence, 4. health and body, 5. the media, 6. politics and law, 7. workplace and economy, 8. childhood and education, and 9. religion.

I've put the items into my own categories - and yes, we are finally back to the '25 problems' format. After a long discussion of Problem 10, Misogyny vs Misandry and Problem 11, the Gender Pay Gap, we'll continue with problems 12-25. I've given them the following names:

12. Yes, That's Annoying,
13. The Weight of History
14. Dickheads Anonymous
15. It's Still Not 1970
16. What Ya Gonna Do?
17. Bullshit or Not?
18. Whinge, Whine, WTF
19. So Fucking What?
20. Stop Caring What People Think
21. Assert Yourself or Die
22. Do Something
23. Give Me My Privilege!
24. Turning Male Problems into Male Privilege
25. Addicted to Feminism

For those not familiar with the format and style of how these privilege lists work, I'll make up a few sample items to give the general idea. Those who want to see the original version can Google the article.

So, these are all the sort of advantages men supposedly enjoy just by being men.

1. You're not expected to have a cheery demeanour, or accused or having 'resting bitch face' if you don't happen to be smiling at a given moment.
2. People don't assume you're stupid and can be taken advantage of when buying a second hand car.
3. You can refuse a date without being thought stuck up, cold, or picky, and without being stalked on social media or in real life.
4. You can go on a bus or into a crowded nightclub without fear of being groped or having your drink spiked.
5. You're allowed to go topless and aren't expected to shave your bodily hair.
6. You can expect to see your gender feature prominently in film and TV roles, especially in the lead.
7. Your temperament and toughness won't be questioned if you run for political office, and you won't be penalised for being childless.

Let's start by conceding that the author is right about some items on her list. My first category is called 'Yes, That's Annoying.'

Problem 12 - Yes, That's Annoying

Some feminists imply that a man could never hope to understand what it's like to be a woman, yet this pessimistic view assumes not only a vast difference between the sexes, but that people have no imagination. Remember also that feminists often comment on what they think life is like for men.

It's not that hard to empathise with other people, especially if some things happen to both genders. Being condescended to, for instance, isn't exclusive to women. I used to go to a badminton club and one day some random guy was my doubles partner. Despite us never having met, he assumed I couldn't play. He suggested I stand up the front near the net for the entire game, leaving the real skill and hard work to him. I declined his 'helpful' suggestion and only just refrained from telling him where he could stick his racquet.

Yes, it is annoying when people you've never met assume you're stupid or incompetent. Of course, this 'everyday sexism' has happened to plenty of women over the years, including in the world of work. So, as in item 115 from the male privilege list, if someone walks into a legal office and assumes the woman behind the desk is the receptionist rather than a lawyer, that's annoying.

When Judge Judy first began in the legal profession, she sat down to lunch with the other judges, all male, and one of them assumed she was the cleaning lady and asked her to leave. As a joke, she started clearing away the dirty cups and plates. The man got angry when he found out the truth because he thought she'd made a fool of him. Judge Judy didn't get the apology she deserved.

Related to this are various points (e.g. 69, 73, 74, and 86) which complain that women are depicted in films and TV as weak, man-centred, or dumb. You'd have to agree it can be annoying to have people of your gender portrayed like that.

In her new book, Clementine Ford complained that growing up as a keen movie watcher, most of the best roles were taken by men, with women relegated to the supporting roles and bit parts. She's right on this point. It would be frustrating, and fair grounds to become a feminist.

Having said that, some of the recent efforts at 'strong female characters' are an overreaction. Rey in *Star Wars* is a blatant 'Mary Sue,' that is, an unrealistically perfect character. Yet Alara from *The Orville* is not, given that she has flaws along with her superhuman strength.

Contrary to what some people think, you can also have a male Mary Sue, sometimes known as a Gary Stu. In the *Red Dwarf* episode, 'Dimension Jump,' Rimmer's alter ego, Ace, is a Gary Stu. Ace is really a parody of a Gary Stu, showing how silly such characters tend to be.

Another recent trend is recasting male roles as women. There's been talk of casting a female James Bond, and a recent theatre production of *Treasure Island* had Jim Hawkins as a girl. The motivation is obvious but that doesn't mean it's a good idea. Both those characters are from the past and should be left alone. The past can't be changed. Whether in fiction or real life, as soon as you start rewriting the past you've become a propagandist.

It's silly to pretend James Bond was a woman. The character is a male from a clear historical context. Perhaps his masculinity would be seen as toxic these days, but that's another story. It should be easy enough to create new strong female roles, like Lisbeth Salander from *The Girl With The Dragon Tattoo*. With so many writers and filmmakers in the world, there's no reason they can't come up with new stories rather than rewriting old ones.

A third example of 'Yes, that's annoying' is item 15 from the MP list, which says that single fathers get more praise for their parenting than do single mothers, who may even be looked down upon. OK, let's concede the point. That could be annoying.

Problem 13 - The Weight of History

Another thing which annoys feminists is that most of history's great achievements were by men. Several items on the MP list point out that history focuses on men's achievements, or that journalism and academic work cites male authors (items 131,

136, 153, 154). In other words, these complaints stem from the fact that for most of history, men had the benefit of more education, power, opportunity etc, which led to them being responsible for most of the achievements we remember.

From a feminist viewpoint, we've got to concede that's pretty annoying. Still, what can you do about it? First, we can agree with the idea that, in principle, if women had had equal access to education in the past, they would have come up with more scientific discoveries, inventions, works of art, and so on.

You are still faced with the problem of the 'weight of history' in that most great achievements were by men. While this is irksome for feminists, the question remains: what can you do about it? Here are three types of responses. Type one is silly, type two sensible but unlikely, and type three sensible and possible.

Silly

1a) Raze civilisation to the ground, erase all our knowledge, and go back to the Stone Age. Then start again with a system of gender equality to give women a fair chance at making the great discoveries.

1b) Rewrite known history and pretend, for example, that gravity wasn't discovered by Isaac Newton, but by Irene Newton.

1c) Vindictively shame and punish men who are alive today as retribution for women being denied chances in the past.

Sensible but unlikely

2a) Stop obsessing over the gender of people who did great things for humanity. Isaac Newton was a man. So what?

2b) Be grateful for what outstanding male scientists, artists, or leaders did for us in the past. They did it for our species as a whole and deserve our thanks.

Sensible and possible

3a) Try to find unsung female heroes from history and give them the praise they missed during their lifetimes.

3b) Forget the past and start doing things now. There's still plenty of great intellectual and artistic work to be done. Most Western women now have equal opportunity to pursue whatever they want, so they should get on with it.

Several items on the MP list allude to the problem of the weight of history. Yes, it is annoying that women were denied opportunities in the past, but that can't be helped. We can only start from where we are now.

There are plenty of other items from the list that may be annoying to women. There's one type that deserves a chapter of its own. It's a category called 'Dickheads Anonymous.'

14

Dickheads Anonymous

Problem 14 – Dickheads Anonymous

My first memory of stupid male behaviour towards girls was as a teenager seeing 1. boys' desire for girls to have sex with them, and 2. boys' disapproval of girls who had sex with them. It seemed silly even at the time.

As mentioned, feminism began for a reason - or rather, several reasons. One was to loosen restrictive gender roles, and another was the bad behaviour of some men towards some women. There are quite a few items of the second type on the male privilege list. Of the 160+ items on the list, about forty fall into this category, so nearly a quarter of the list is about bad behaviour by men. These range from irritating (telling women to smile) to irksome (fat shaming, sexual harassment) to evil (rape and violence).

It is odd to see bad or foolish behaviour described as some kind of male privilege. Perhaps the 'privilege' lies in the idea that men don't experience it from each other. In that case, women should be assured that the idiocy of other men *can* also be bestowed on their brothers, in ways to which women are often immune. In that sense, here's an example of 'female privilege.'

> You can walk into a bar without being challenged to a fight by a random drunk because you were 'looking at him.'

I therefore find solidarity with my feminist sisters on the basis of having felt the harassment of male idiots. So, let's move on to the quarter of our list's complaints that make up the category of Dickheads Anonymous.

To start at the low end of the scale, our list says that women are often interrupted, told to smile, or expected to step aside if a man is walking in their path (items 2, 7, and 10). If true, this is indeed a violation of basic good manners.

Then there's point no. 3 which claims women are often assumed not to know what they're talking about. If that's true, it does raise a couple of questions: who are you hanging out with? And why? Are we talking about the fictional 1950s TV world of *Mad Men*, or the real world of 2019? If 2019, then to repeat: who are you hanging out with? And why?

Point 3 also mentions 'mansplaining.' But as the entire male privilege list - all 167 items - is an attempt to explain to men how lucky they are, this seems rather hypocritical.

There are also quite a few points in the list about body issues. Among them are slimming and hair removal.

There's a type of man one might describe as a 'fatophobe.' Apparently that's a word now. It means someone with a strong dislike of body weight. We're not talking of obesity, but the sort of voluptuousness that's been thought attractive at different times in history.

A few years ago I had a young male flatmate who was on the dating site Tinder. Every now and then, he'd hold up his phone to show the photo of a dating prospect. Almost every time, he would remark that she'd be really hot if only she wasn't so fat. I'd peer into his phone and see a girl of quite normal weight.

To add to the awkwardness, my girlfriend of the time was genuinely overweight, but as she hardly ever came to my place (I went to hers), the flatmate hadn't met her. I'd say to him, 'Well, my girlfriend is overweight. It's not that important, you know.' He'd sort of laugh absently, as if unable to process this information. Then the next day he'd show me another photo of some 'horribly overweight' (i.e. normal sized) girl on Tinder.

Beyond the basics of physical health, the topic of weight gets far too much attention. If all the time spent thinking about weight went into developing the mind, how much further advanced our society would be! And if there are hordes of men policing the fatophobe regime, they're all paid up members of Dickheads Anonymous, so why would you go out with them anyway?

There's also the recent ridiculous trend of full Brazilian waxes, a scourge imposed on society by the Dickheads Anonymous army along with the 'beauty industry.' Women capitulated to this trend with shameful rapidity, which is their fault as well. No one forced them.

Sexual Assault

But these are minor issues. When it comes to more serious offences - from the unethical right up to actual evil - what can you say, except the obvious? There's a lot in the male privilege list about sexual harassment - at least ten items - and more items about rape and violence. Of course, no one is going to condone blatant harassment, rape, or violence.

When it comes to rape and the threat of sexual assault, this is clearly one area of life where women are worse off than men. Each day, women are aware of the possibility of sexual assault. The limits this puts on behaviour are explained, for example, in Soraya Chemaly's book *Rage Becomes Her*.

While women are worse off in this respect and deserve sympathy, why describe it as 'male privilege'? Better to call it female disadvantage, which it is, rather than imply that being less likely to be raped is some kind of perk.

The last couple of years have seen some well publicised rape /murders of women in Australia. In the aftermath, some feminists have tried to impose a collective shame on men as a class. This will be discussed in chapter 18, 'A Dream of Fecunda.'

One thing's for sure, when it comes to topics like 'rape culture' and the Me Too movement, there's a level of zeal that exceeds all others. This makes it important to not just listen to feminists, but more moderate voices. Janice Fiamengo has a number of excellent YouTube videos on these topics. Feminist and rape survivor, Wendy McElroy, gave a strong speech criticizing the idea of rape culture, which is also on YouTube. Back in the 1990s, Helen Garner's book, *The First Stone*, looked at a case study of sexual harassment and some of its points still apply.

Online Abuse

Suppose there's a hypothetical feminist who is accused of hating men, and she's on Twitter and Facebook. There's a type of man that just gives her ammo, fuelling and justifying whatever misandry is actually there. This is the type of guy who, instead of offering reasoned arguments, just makes nasty personal attacks.

Anyone who is a public activist knows they are a target, but there are different types of attacks. Let's say there are three main levels of communication in which people argue with each other.

Level one is calm discussion of ideas, and may even entail people trying to understand each other. This is what used to happen in universities long ago, but it's rare these days.

Level two is mainly about dismissing someone with an abusive label. The left side of politics is notorious for using labels instead of arguments: racist, misogynist, Nazi, Islamophobe, and so on. In recent years, the right side of politics has adopted its own terms: cuckservative, social justice warrior, etc. A particularly good one, 'NPC,' was all over Twitter in late 2018. Meaning 'non player character,' it was aimed at those who mindlessly parrot PC opinions. Level two attacks have their place and to some degree are part of the rich tapestry of the culture war.

Level three attacks, however, are just nasty personal abuse. Although there's a place for 'sledging' which has some actual wit, references to someone's looks, weight, family, etc, have no relevance or value. So, if some dickhead goes on Twitter and calls a feminist a 'fucking ugly bitch' or whatever, (as some apparently do), that is no use to anybody.

A person tweeting this just makes himself look stupid and nasty, and justifies whatever misandry his target already has. In summary, the tweeter is a full member of Dickheads Anonymous and does no good for any cause, certainly not men's.

The point of the present chapter is to agree that one reason feminism exists is to protest the bad behaviour of some men towards some women. Whether or not it is systemic is another question, and feminists rarely acknowledge that there is also a lot of bad behaviour going the other way. There's no doubt there are plenty of dickheads out there. Along with the abusers, the harassers, and the fatophobes, there *are* some men who never do any housework, assume women are stupid, or whatever else.

OK - so there have been, and still are, quite a few dickheads out there. Maybe even a lot if you really want to look for them. But if feminism is composed of the vast and the spurious, it's time to look at the spurious part of the equation. While feminism is right about some things, it's wrong about plenty more - and it's time to get rid of the dead wood from this ideological belief system.

15

Whinge, Whine, WTF

The next three chapters take a more skeptical look at items from the male privilege list. The first category is items which seem out of date.

Problem 15 – It's Still Not 1970

The male privilege list being used was published in 2016, but some of its points belong in the 1970s. Point 4, for instance, is about sexist language but of the examples given, the word 'mankind' doesn't get much airplay anymore. As for 'foreman,' that must be one of the few job titles not to have gone gender-neutral.

Point 29 about having to take the husband's name in marriage is also pretty retro. There's no compulsion to get married these days, or take the man's name if you do.

Then there are some points about childhood and education. Item 141 says boys receive more educational toys, which open up career ideas for them, while girls often get toys related to beauty, housework, and parenting. Definitely right in 1969 - but in 2019? Girls are getting plenty of educational toys these days. Even if they're still getting some of the other sort, there can't be many girls in 2019 who think their career options are limited to beauty, housework, and parenting.

If we do want to influence girls away from that, perhaps we should look higher and stop giving fame to reality stars, models, and beauty bloggers. At the time of writing, Kim Kardashian has 60 million followers on Twitter. Perhaps it's because she got beauty-related toys as a child. If only she'd been given a toy telescope, she might be one of our top scientists by now.

If you believe item 148, being boisterous is encouraged in boys but not in girls. If that were true, it would be unfair, but there's good reason to doubt it. Most primary school teachers are women and it's a real stretch to think all those teachers are shushing girls. On the other hand, quite a few boys are being given ADHD drugs to dampen their energetic natures. In her book, *The War on Boys*, Christina Hoff Sommers cites a psychologist, Michael Thompson, who thinks girl behaviour in schools is seen as 'the gold standard' and boys are viewed as 'defective girls.'

In line with this, the next two items on our list are not just out of date, but rather selective in how they've been perceived. Points 146 and 147 say boys get more attention in school. They're often asked to answer questions even when not raising their hands, and get more teacher feedback overall.

First, it seems highly doubtful teachers are ignoring girls in favour of boys. Why would they? I recently did some teaching training myself, and teachers are trained in equity - that is, allowing all students to have a fair go at school. A teacher who was found to be favouring boys would be quickly censured.

Second, if boys are being given more attention, it's mainly because they're falling so far behind. Girls are now doing better than boys in school and get more places at university. So, as for getting more teacher attention, the likely reason is very different than supposed. To take an example from pop culture, if bright Lisa Simpson is first to raise her hand at every question and dim Bart is skulking in silence up the back, the teacher is calling on Bart to stop him sliding further into decline.

In the pressure of a crowded classroom, the bright kids often receive less teacher attention, because they need it the least. It's the struggling kids who get more time and feedback. With boys doing poorly at school, to interpret more teacher attention as some kind of bounty is a bit perverse. This item could have gone into my Problem 24 category, 'Turning male problems into male privilege.' It suggests the need to hold on to a victim narrative even when your team is actually winning.

Then there are some points about money. Item 123 mentions 'financial abuse,' where women are stuck in bad relationships with abusive men but can't escape because of financial dependence. If this is meant to be some kind of quintessential point about the plight of Western women, it's one drawn from the world of 1870 rather than 1970.

While there *are* women in this position, plenty of men are also stuck in bad marriages over money. That's not from depending on women's income, but in knowing they'll take a major financial hit if they leave. Countless relationships have soured at some point after marriage and children. The decline may be fast or slow, and from a legal standpoint the reasons don't matter. If the man is unhappy and wants out, he'll pay a heavy price. That's one reason men stay in unhappy marriages, and a reason some are now refusing to marry in the first place. So to suggest 'financial abuse' in bad relationships only goes one way is wrong.

A less drastic point about money is item 109, which says that if you're a man, you're not expected to check with your partner before taking a promotion. There's a more basic issue here. *Any* reasonable person should check with their partner before taking a promotion.

Let's say a man came home one day and said, 'Starting Monday I'm working twenty more hours a week. I'll be home at 9pm and working Saturdays. You'll have to quit your job and do all the parenting - and by the way, we're moving to Florida.' If you're married to a man like that, you've got bigger problems than gender inequality. You're married to a narcissist.

In other words, communicating about life changing decisions isn't a privilege for either sex. It's simple good manners.

Problem 16 - What Ya Gonna Do?

In the fictional world of *The Sopranos*, mafia boss, Tony Soprano was a potent force. Yet sometimes events were bigger than him. It might be a failed business enterprise, the loss of a colleague, or even the sudden death of his own mother. So there was Tony, usually at yet another funeral, as one of his mafia buddies offered words of commiseration. Upon which, Tony would adopt a world-weary expression, shrug, raise an eyebrow and say, 'What Ya Gonna Do?'

Some things you just can't control. For example, we all suffer from aging. Indeed, to jump from the mafia to Buddhism, it was the sight of an old beggar which shocked the young Buddha into realising we all get old and die. Yet even within this indiscriminate curse, women feel discriminated against. Item 56 says men get better with age while women decline.

Whether this is even true or not, whose fault is it? Oh, that's right - nobody's. So why make it yet another reason to resent men? If it makes women feel better, in two of the other great certainties of life, men will probably die sooner and pay more taxes out of all their privileged income.

Point 66 is an odd one. Apparently it's a privilege that men are allowed to show their nipples in public, an option denied to women. So what ya gonna do, walk around topless in public?

This isn't a privilege so much as an annoyance. I'm all for equal rights here. Not in that women should also display their nipples in public (fine in theory, perhaps not in practice), but that men should stop doing it. In Australia in summer, you can hardly go out in public without show ponies parading their naked torsos on every street corner. A nipple ban would be fine by me. My feminist comrades, I stand (clothed) shoulder to shoulder with you on this one.

Problem 17 - Bullshit or Not?

One of the strangest items on the male privilege list is number 145 which claims that girls get higher grades if they're attractive. This is apparently a terrible handicap because it tells girls that they are valued for their looks, not their minds. It also means that girls' grades depend on their appearance.

Almost all men would agree that *their* grades don't depend on appearance, but on performance. As this is exactly how it should be, it makes no sense to call it a privilege. You'd hope girls are treated exactly the same. But if you take this odd item at face value, surely it can only be female privilege if girls get higher grades for attractiveness. Somehow, an unfair advantage has been turned into yet more injustice for women.

Suppose there is a girl who gets high grades and is also attractive. If so, one of the following is true:

a) She got those grades fairly because she deserved them for the work, and would be rightly annoyed if anyone said otherwise.

b) She got the grades unfairly and doesn't know.

c) She got the grades unfairly, knows, but doesn't care.

d) She got the grades unfairly, both knows and cares, and demands a lower grade from the teacher.

The only one to experience injustice would be the first girl for the implication she wasn't worth the high grade. The second girl would be ignorant, the third immoral, and the fourth moral. Still, let's say you took one hundred attractive girls with high grades, there would be plenty in the first three groups and almost none in the fourth.

Whatever else it is, it's hard to see how this bizarre item is actually a form of *male* privilege.

Then there's point 156 which alleges that college professors are more likely to answer inquiries from male students, especially white ones, than from anyone else. Presumably, this means questions during class.

This is another out of date idea. It may have been true thirty years ago, but universities are now dominated by left wing progressives, and few professors would *dare* to not answer inquiries from women, especially black women.

It's quite hard to visualise point 156 in action. Are there really lecture rooms where white males are answered when they raise their hands, but black women are ignored if they do the same? Even in the case of multiple hands going up at once, it's hard to see a professor getting this wrong. With universities full of identity politics, professors can be sacked for any perceived sin - and who would refuse to answer inquiries from black or female students?

Or are we talking about the kind of 'inquiries' seen during the Chinese Cultural Revolution, where teachers were surrounded by mobs of angry students. You get those in the West now too. If these are the sort of inquiries professors aren't answering, it's because it's hard to answer thirty inquiries at once, especially when they come with the threat of violence.

Moving to the field of politics, point 89 says that if a woman fails to be voted into public office, it may be because of her gender.

If this is really a disadvantage, you'd have to wonder why some female candidates make gender a big part of their campaign. At one of Hillary Clinton's 2016 rallies, Madeleine Albright implied female voters should vote for her *because* of her gender. Clinton's loss hasn't deterred other female candidates, including women of colour, from making their identity central to their election hopes.

There's also item 91, which claims female candidates' appearance gets more attention than their abilities, and other items implying a woman has a far tougher time in politics than a man.

First, if a woman is running for high office, even actual *misogynists* would care more about her abilities than her looks. They may not like her looks, but it's her policies that would affect them.

Second, *all* candidates will be scrutinized for their appearance. In some cases, this may even work to their advantage. Barack Obama, for example, had a brilliant appearance. He was a handsome, well dressed African-American, and an eloquent speaker. Yet he also misled Americans about the gender pay gap. Thomas Sowell, a black, conservative intellectual, said 'Obama's political genius is his ability to say things that will sound good to people who have not followed the issues in any detail - regardless of how obviously fraudulent what he says may be to those who have.'

Obama had a good run with the press. So, is it true female politicians are more harshly scrutinized? The media has been pretty kind to Jacinda Ardern, New Zealand's prime minister. Some in the Australian media can't stop gushing about her. She is also photogenic, which has undoubtedly worked in her favour. As for Hillary Clinton, she did receive harsh treatment, some of which may have stemmed from misogyny.

Having said that, there's no doubt which politician has had the nastiest treatment of recent times, and that is Donald Trump. Since the 2016 election, it has been an eye opener to witness the torrent of vitriol directed at Trump, both in the media and on social media. It has been a sustained campaign of hatred that hasn't let up for over three years.

There was even an unflattering naked statue of Trump on public display in Los Angeles for a while in 2016. Visitors took delight in photographing themselves mocking the statue. Whatever anyone thinks of Trump, this was pretty despicable, and there's no way Hillary Clinton would have been treated like that. In light of this, among other things, it's hard to take seriously the claim women are more harshly treated or scrutinized than men in politics.

Trump is the target of leftist ire for many reasons, one of which is that he is white and male. According to feminist theory, that should make him an apex predator, enjoying an abundance of privilege in how he is treated. Yet the sheer vitriol directed at him shows that the idea is long out of date.

Problem 18 – Whinge, Whine, WTF

We now move onto a section of hearty whining which offers a smorgasbord of interest, and it's hard not to be flippant when discussing it. We're getting into some weird territory at this point.

Take item 13 on the list, which claims car salesmen take advantage of women and offer them worse prices than male customers. If true, this does show dreadful sexism from car sellers in assuming females know nothing about cars. Still, rather than slander second hand car salesmen - who *never* rip off men, by the way - let's speak more broadly about scammers in general.

From all reports, the scamming industry actually has an equal opportunity policy. It's a model industry in that regard. You see, scammers don't care if you're black or white, male or female, straight or gay. As long as you have money, they'll happily accept you as a client.

Let's say some privileged white man went over to a struggling third world country. As soon as he stepped off the plane, he'd get a warm welcome from the scamming industry.

Do you think any local businessman from the scamming trade is going to see him and think, 'Look at that smug bastard with his white male privilege. I'm not taking *his* money'?

On the contrary, those paragons of equality would take the guy's dough and put it with the gender-neutral money they take from all the other demographics.

Mind you, if it turns out scammers *do* target women more than men, that is definitely sexist. The government should take a firm stand on sexism in the scamming industry, and any crook caught targeting women should have his or her license revoked.

There's also a bit about housework in the male privilege list. This vintage item from the golden age of feminism has been covered in the GPG chapters, but it turns out the domestic labour issue is pretty old hat. According to item 34, there's also something called 'emotional labour,' and women are expected to do more of it in relationships with men. Now granted, my first thought was *what the fuck is emotional labour*? Having looked it up, it was a letdown to find it's mostly just normal stuff people do already - like managing their emotions, other people's emotions, and the complexities of daily life.

Still, this isn't just a domestic matter, as emotional labour is rampant in the workplace too. Item 139 says part of emotional labour is preserving office harmony. It seems much of this falls on women, who are expected to take on this work in addition to their 'day job' (the actual job), yet receive no compensation for it. Presumably that means money.

This is a tough one to sort out. First, you'd have to find a way to put a fiscal value on emotional labour. What if Bruce from accounts gets a rude email from his boss? We can see his ears reddening as he reads it. 'That's it!' he exclaims. 'I'm gonna quit.'

Now suppose Heather at the next desk interrupts her busy schedule to say, 'Don't take it personally, Bruce, he's under a lot of pressure from head office.' So tell me - is that worth five bucks or ten? If she gets him a glass of water - is that twenty? What if she has a discreet word to the boss as well? That's gotta be worth fifty, or at least an employee of the month award.

Still, in the equal opportunity Utopia we're building, you'd have to let men in on the act. If Bruce puts in the hard yards and reciprocates Heather's caring, you have to reward him too. It's not like we're living in the 1950s when men notoriously got away with doing no emotional labour as well as no housework.

Finally, what about Courtney at the next desk, whose only skill is *disrupting* office harmony? She's one of those workplace psychopaths you hear about (members in both genders) whose main work activities are bullying, backstabbing, delegating, and taking credit for others' work. If Heather gets a bonus for her efforts, does Courtney get a fine? The brave new world of emotional labour definitely needs some thought.

Problem 19 - So Fucking What?

I must admit the tone of this chapter has gone downhill. Rest assured some decorum will soon be restored. But first, there's one more piece of useful rudeness to apply.

In November, 2018, there was a report on the serious lack of gender equality in the field of jazz music. It turns out most jazz musicians are male. One lobby group said there would be a concerted effort to achieve gender parity in the next four years. That is, to have the same number of women as men playing jazz by 2022.

At this point, there's one response that may help alleviate the crisis in jazz. You see, it's absolutely true there are more men than women in jazz. Yet there's one response which could tackle the problem head on, possibly even fixing it for good. It's a three word slogan we should all keep in mind.

So Fucking What?

Playing jazz isn't for everyone. Plenty of people don't even like this style of music. Of those who do, a minority will want to play it. A further subsection of that minority will have the skill and the will to do it professionally.

More to the point, let's personify jazz for a moment. Jazz doesn't care who plays it, and jazz especially doesn't care what sort of genitals they have. It's irrelevant. Jazz fans shouldn't care either.

As for whether girls and boys should have the same chance to learn the art form, sure, but let's not confuse equality of opportunity with equality of outcome.

There's a style of music - heavy metal - which has even less gender equality. Is this yet another crisis? Should bands like Slayer, Black Sabbath, and Judas Priest have had female members?

What about classical music, a genre in which women are far more prevalent. Does it matter if there's a 70-30 split in favour of either gender in the makeup of a given symphony orchestra? Certainly not to me.

The fixation on gender balance is getting rather absurd. As YouTube commentator Dave Cullen said, it's getting to the stage where buses will refuse to pick up passengers if it spoils a fifty-fifty gender split on the bus. Some lonely guy will be waiting at the stop, only to be told, 'Sorry, we've got eight men and eight women at the moment. You can't get on unless one of your lot gets off.'

There are far better things our buses could be doing, such as displaying giant three word slogans that can help fix the crisis in jazz. Yes, there *are* more men than women in jazz. It's a calamity. What's more, there are all sorts of disasters like that at the moment, because some fields of endeavour have more men in them, and some fields have more women. So here's my suggestion for a major new advertising campaign to tackle the crisis head on. Let's put it up in capital letters on the side of all our buses. It's a fantastic slogan of just three little words.

So Fucking What?

16
Stop Caring What People Think

According to the male privilege list, there's an invisible force which shapes the lives of women and makes them obsess over weight, spend lots of money on clothes and makeup, be bad at maths and science, take jobs in customer service, or have children and quit their jobs to raise them. This invisible force is called 'Social Expectations.' Under patriarchy, it acts like a force of gravity to make women do things - which presumably they wouldn't otherwise do.

It is true Social Expectations can exert major force on people to do things that aren't good for them. Consider the millions of young men who went to war in 1914. They were expected to give their lives. Those who refused were called cowards by other men, and by the women who gave them white feathers. This sort of public shaming helped persuade them that running into machine gun fire was the right thing to do. If people can be compelled to do something as insane as that, you can't deny Social Expectations can be pretty damn powerful.

There's also a weird phenomenon called the Abilene paradox which shows how people sometimes conform against their own wishes, because they think group consensus has been reached. An article by Harinam and Henderson explains:

> Imagine a group of people trying to make dinner plans. One person suggests driving to a restaurant in a distant city called Abilene. Another person, not wanting to travel very far but dreading an argument, says "sure." A third individual, now thinking that her two peers want to go to Abilene, doesn't want to be the odd person out. She agrees that Abilene is a good

idea. This domino effect leads to everyone thinking everyone else wants to go to Abilene when in fact a consensus does not exist.

This is called The Abilene Paradox...It consists of individuals who do not agree with an idea yet acquiesce because of their mistaken belief that a consensus has been reached.

Why is any of this important? Well, if enough people falsify their preferences then many of us will begin to mistake polite but dishonest assent for the honest truth.

Suppose you and I publicly supported a policy we privately despised. If neither of us publicly dissents then we'll continue to openly support this policy, making it more plausible than it actually is. And neither of us benefits when our "support" for this policy paves the way for its implementation.

According to feminism, women's behaviour is also largely controlled by the weight of Social Expectations. Although not as extreme as when men practiced mandatory suicide in the war, a complex network of pressures does help to shape behaviour. This may be true, but how much of Social Expectations are Abilene paradoxes where people think agreement has been reached when it hasn't?

There's a fine line to walk when approaching the idea that Social Expectations are our master. We must be aware we're being brainwashed to a greater or lesser degree, but to then deny any part in caving to social pressure is simply not honest. This gets back to Karen Straughan's theory of agents and objects.

Some feminists imply that women have no agency, thus no responsibility. They are just 'objects' pushed around by external forces. Therefore it's not up to women to fix themselves, it's up to external forces - society as a whole - to change so that women can be free.

While Social Expectations can be powerful, it's really up to individuals to resist social pressure rather than blaming it for everything that happens to them. The problem is a lot of people care far too much about pleasing others and doing what is socially acceptable.

A big part of overcoming this would be to adopt the slogan 'Stop Caring What People Think.' The next three problems address this in terms of 1. appearance, 2. behaviour, and 3. life choices and abilities. At the risk of sounding flippant, you can get closer to happiness by following the SAD formula:

1. Stop caring what people think.
2. Assert yourself or die.
3. Do something.

Problem 20 – Stop Caring What People think

Several items on the male privilege list complain that women are 'judged' for looking or behaving a certain way. While this is true, the best response is to stop caring. Of course, 1970s feminists told women to stop conforming to Social Expectations, so this is nothing new. Yet as the male privilege list I'm using came out in 2016, it seems this is still somehow men's fault.

Several items complain that women are expected to wear certain kinds of clothes and makeup, be slim, shave their body hair, etc. Adopting the mantra 'stop caring what people think' would help solve most of these problems.

One of the many things women are being 'forced' to do by the patriarchy is spend thousands of dollars on over-priced clothes and makeup. While the clothing and makeup industries have some responsibility, the patriarchy's biggest foot soldiers here are women. It is not straight, white men who read Worst Dressed lists or think it's a *faux pas* to wear the same outfit twice in five years. How strange that the so-called beneficiaries of patriarchy aren't the ones enforcing it. Perhaps it's unfair to blame men for what the Triviality Police are doing to each other.

A lot of people *like* clothes and makeup. *Project Runway*, after all, is one of the more entertaining reality TV shows. Those who enjoy fancy clothes and makeup shouldn't complain. Those who don't, need not partake. Stop caring what people think.

As journalist, Tracy Spicer, said in her recent TED talk, women could achieve so much more if they stopped trying to conform to other people's inflated expectations of how they should look, and directed the energy into more worthwhile pursuits.

The key word is 'conform.' You can't cave to all this social pressure then see it as male privilege. Better to stop being a herd animal and doing what everyone else is doing. The other key word is 'achieve.' Maybe there *would* be more female CEOs and Nobel laureates if they stopped caring what others think.

As for weight, who really cares? Yes, people may be healthier and more attractive if they're slim, but there are more important things to think about. Unless you're desperate to please the fatophobes, your weight isn't that interesting.

When it comes to body hair, there's a recent example of over-caring what people think. Sometime round the turn of the century, the idea was put about that Bush was bad and had to go. No, not the president, female pubic hair. Whether this was started by the beauty industry, the neuroses industry, or the Institute for Male Privilege, who knows, but the idea caught on.

So, to 'objectify' the female body for a moment, the triangular pubic bush which had been a visually erotic highlight for centuries, was now pronounced bad. Pubic hair was suddenly being shaved and waxed left, right, and centre as this ridiculous trend caught on. Women, in the attempt to be sexually attractive, made themselves less sexually attractive by shaving their pubic hair.

Whose fault is it all this pain and bother was visited on modern women? To a small degree the men who allegedly liked it, but mainly the women themselves for caving to social pressure, fashion, and trends. They did it because everyone else was. So the silly trend of the full Brazilian wax, previously a minority fetish, became a mainstream expectation.

We're all influenced by the weight of social pressure, but come on. Stop being a sheep. Stop being mindless.

Stop caring what people think.

Problem 21 – Assert Yourself or Die

Apparently it's also male privilege that women find it hard to ask for pay rises, are interrupted more, and are expected to do more domestic labour at home and emotional labour in the office (items 2, 34, 35, 129, 139 on the list).

While these issues may be annoying, it's up to people to assert themselves. To take one example, when I first went to university, tute groups were dominated by confident, extroverted types who seemed to have an advantage making their voices heard. But it would be pointless to see this as their privilege and sit there angrily while they spoke. For more introverted people like myself, you can either speak up and join in, or sit there silently fuming about extrovert privilege.

This problem is being dealt with very briefly, and of course it isn't as simple as I'm making out - but basically, if you want any kind of social power you have to assert yourself to some degree. If there's a major power imbalance, that's different, but in a normal home or work environment, you have to speak up.

If you dislike the way things are done or how you're expected to behave, it won't help to suffer in silence, harbour secret resentment, and call it someone else's privilege. One of this book's earlier chapters was called 'Complaining is Not a Strategy,' but there's a difference between complaining and negotiation. It's up to individuals to say what they want, and negotiate better conditions. If that doesn't work they can leave, if it matters that much.

If other people see this assertiveness as 'bossy' or 'aggressive' (item 142), so what? Stop caring what people think.

Assert yourself or die.

Problem 22 – Do Something

If we believe the male privilege list, women are also coerced into being bad at maths and science, or unfunny as comedians. They're conned into working in the 'female professions,' and face the curse of getting more attention for their looks or relationships than their achievements (items 82, 133, 138, 149).

Reading these items, you almost get the sense women have no say over anything that happens to them. They're just blown about by the winds of the patriarchy. Again, while this may be true under the Taliban, in the fictional Republic of Gilead, or in the Western world of 1870, it isn't true for most Western women in 2019.

No one is stopping women from being good at maths and science, or funny as comedians. No one is making them train for and enter the 'female professions.' No one's making them focus on looks instead of achievements.

The privilege list complains women are more likely to work in domestic labour jobs (item 111) or people-pleasing roles such as flight attendants. If those flight attendants don't like their jobs, why did they train for them? Perhaps their planes are flying to Abilene.

That's not to say working conditions in various professions can't be improved, or people don't start their careers over-optimistically before being let down - but that's a different topic.

It's also male privilege that men are valued more for their work achievements than their marriage (item 133), and get more praise for their abilities than their appearance (143).

This is again out of date. The feminist influence in education has seen huge amounts of encouragement given to girls for their abilities and achievements.

Yet even if the MP list was right and girls were still being held back, there comes a time to say 'Enough!' At some point you have to stop complaining about being prevented from doing things... and do something.

You can talk all day about what you're expected to do or not expected to do. Eventually you have to decide to do something.

In summary, the quest for happiness can be pursued by following the three step SAD formula:

1. Stop caring what people think.
2. Assert yourself or die.
3. Do something.

Who knows? Maybe it will work. It's worth a try.

17
Give Me My Privilege!

Problem 23 – Give Me My Privilege!

Back in the last century, there was a new version of the Bible called *Good News For Modern Man*. It was all about the blessings given to people by Christianity. What has this to do with feminism? Well, so far this book has spoken about male privilege like it's a bad thing. What has been overlooked is the wonderful news feminists bring men. Just like that new version of the Bible, they bring 'Good News For Modern Man!' It turns out we can win at life just by being born, thanks to all the special perks we get.

For example, take item 120 on the list. It turns out men can build their careers by using "good ol' boy" networks. Well why wasn't I told? Can the author of the list please forward me the good ol' boys' names and addresses? As someone who's hopeless at networking, it would be a real boon!

It would especially help in my quest to be a writer. According to item 72, writers of my gender are far more likely to be published and promoted in the book trade. On first reading this, I was overjoyed! It was only later I realised with a shock that my work is still fairly unknown. Tell you what, it's an awful letdown for a chap to find out he's got white male privilege, and *still* can't get his book onto the top tables of Kinokuniya beside Clem's. (That's Australia's biggest bookshop, in case you don't know.)

It's a 'funny game,' publishing. It started off in Australia as a simple purveyor of stories and information. There was a wild anything-goes period in the 1970s when anyone could get published. Then in the '90s, it all got a bit serious. It was a time of victim vendettas and affirmative action, when the old male priv regime got shunted aside for a while. You could barely walk into a bookshop without tripping over empowering tales of trauma and oppression. Victims of the world were uniting to get their voices heard. In hindsight, you'd have to say they were dark days for male privilege, because action got so affirmative it led to Wanda Koolmatrie.

This story has become legend in the book world, but apparently it's all true. Back in the mid-90s some wannabe author was trying to get published. He was a white male and all, so he should have had some priv points in the bank. Trouble was, it just wasn't happening for him. By all accounts, he pretty much walked into every publishing house in Australia. But no matter how many times he went into head office and pulled out his white penis, they still wouldn't give him the publishing deal he'd earned just by being born.

I don't know the full ins and outs of it but, long story short, he sent in another manuscript under the pen name Wanda Koolmatrie. 'Wanda' was an aboriginal lady and the book was about her struggle as part of the stolen generation. Did Wanda get published? Did she what! She even won a literary award and had her book studied in school.

There was a brief hoo-hah when it came out that Wanda was really a white male, then the author faded back into obscurity. You've got to feel for him. From time to time he must have lain awake nights wondering why the height of his white male privilege was that brief time when he was black and female.

Those political days are gone now. With the financial squeeze on the book industry, publishing is once again a simple purveyor of stories and information - but only if they sell. In light of that, there's only one kind of privilege that counts in publishing now. Excuse the jargon, but it's 'platform privilege.' In the common tongue, it means fame. In these tough economic times, the only thing that matters for authors is being well known to the public, say, by being on TV, a star on social media, or writing regular columns for *The Age* or *Sydney Morning Herald*.

The power of platform privilege is shown by the fact that even non-authors can become authors if they have platform. A young beauty blogger named Zoella had a hit with her groundbreaking *Girl Online* novel. It turned out to have been ghost-written by some other girl, but as Zoella had a million YouTube followers, she was the one with the book deal. The model, Cara Delevingne, put out a similar type of book, also ghost-written, although she did contribute some plot ideas. As you can see, platform privilege is so powerful it can magically turn non-authors into authors, especially if they're young, famous, and pretty.

White male privilege - you've gotta love it. It's wonderful to hear the news of how powerful men really are. Without feminism, we would never have known.

And the good news doesn't stop there. According to the MP list, men don't get harassed on the internet (item 83), can be reckless with money with little blame (124), and can have strong political views without being disapproved of or called nasty names (100).

That last item is especially good news. It's a relief to know that after publication of this book, I won't be called a misogynist, Nazi, white supremacist, or any of the other labels you get these days for having the wrong views.

Thank God for male privilege - it's the gift that keeps on giving. Thank feminists for letting us know. Just like that new version of the Bible, they bring us 'Good News For Modern Man!'

Problem 24 – Turning Male Problems Into Male Privilege

To continue this theme, men are so blessed that under the feminist gaze even male *problems* turn into male privilege.

For instance, male nerds were until recently seen as low status losers. Not anymore. Point 14 on the MP list says that if men are rejected by mainstream society they can find acceptance in nerd groups, but female nerds are kept out of those groups too. So being a low status loser can actually become a sort of *privilege* for male nerds.

Or how about single fathers? You might think their lives are quite hard, but according to point 113, single mother households tend to be poorer and worse off. It may be technically true, but imagine a single father being a figure of *envy*.

Then there's item 30 about Viagra helping impotent men maintain their sex lives, when there's no such product for women. Fancy that - an embarrassing male condition is not really a problem, it's a privilege.

Are you seeing a pattern? Name a problem - any problem - experienced by men, and under the feminist gaze, it's actually a privilege because women will always be worse off in any area of life. Agony: much worse than yours.

That must explain Hillary Clinton's infamous statement about women having always been the primary victims of war. You see, men being shot by machine guns or blown up isn't so much a problem for them as for their wives - because their selfish act of being killed has left their women the job of getting by without them. The comment is from a speech Clinton gave in 1998 at a domestic violence conference in El Salvador. It must have seemed like a good idea in that context, but translates poorly outside of it.

Some of the other points are hard to reconcile. Point 148 says that energetic behaviour is excused in boys, yet point 65 is about getting better treatment for ADHD. Some of the symptoms of ADHD may be the same energetic behaviour listed in point 148. So this 'energy' isn't really being excused, it's being treated with drugs. It's hard to tell if this is a problem or a privilege.

Anyhow, enough about how awesome life is for men. Let's finish this chapter by taking another look at Problem 4 - Female Privilege. I've followed the same style and format as the male privilege list, even using some of the same categories: social norms, politics, and so on. I've got to admit some of these items are pretty silly, but that's where we end up when it comes to a bitch-fest about whose agony is the worst.

Female Privilege

Social Norms

1. You can pursue 'feminine' interests without people assuming you're homosexual or doing it to impress women.
2. As your gender is encouraged to talk about feelings and establish friendship groups, you're likely to have a stronger support network in times of crisis. Feminists claim this is an example of how 'patriarchy hurts men too.' Fine - so we can admit women enjoy some privilege in the current system.
3. If you're wrong in an argument, you can maintain a self righteous tone and deny it, but a male is expected to 'man up' and admit when he's mistaken. (Mind you, plenty of men don't live up to this principle either.)
4. You can verbally attack someone, then claim harassment if the person calls you out on it or fights back.

Sex and Relationships

5. On average, you are the more attractive and sexually desired gender.
6. You feel entitled to make a long 'shopping list' of traits you want in your dream man, even if you may offer little in return, then later complain you can't meet the right guy.
7. If you choose to and are ethically OK with it, you can use your sexuality for financial gain as a sex worker, or by attracting a wealthy mate. (This obviously doesn't refer to women coerced into sex work against their consent.)
8. If you're married and happen to be financially supported by your partner, you're not considered abnormal or a sponge.
9. You can sustain a loving sexual relationship for a short period, then after marriage and baby, lose interest in your partner. If he doesn't like it, too bad, because he's now legally and financially bound to you and your child. You can also use the holy badge of motherhood to ward off any accusations of selfishness.
10. If you marry a man on a much higher salary than your own and later divorce, you'll walk away from the marriage with far more money than you entered it, regardless of the reasons for the divorce.

Violence and Harassment

11. You're less likely to be the victim of violence.
12. You can walk into a bar without being challenged to a fight by some random drunk because you were 'looking at him.'

13. If you choose to, you can flirt in the workplace or social settings without fear of being accused of harassment.
14. In some cases of domestic violence, you can physically attack your partner, knowing he will be arrested and charged if he retaliates.

The Media and other Institutions

15. If you're attractive, your 'beauty privilege' can help you get a job as a TV presenter. Years later, you can complain about sexism when replaced by someone else hired for the same reason.
16. Your narrative of female victimisation is accepted by media, universities, and government. Those who question it will be attacked or ignored. Meanwhile, you can complain women are an embattled minority fighting the establishment.
17. You can use your privileged positions in media and universities to attack men's rights activists knowing they have no access to the same institutional power to answer back or make their case.
18. You can vilify the entire opposite sex without being called out on your sexism.
19. You can make long lists about male privilege, while rarely mentioning female privilege. You can cherry-pick data that supports your beliefs, while ignoring data that doesn't.
20. Thanks to identity politics, you can blame all the world's problems on white males, at the same time enjoying all the comfort and convenience of a world largely created by white males.

Politics and Law

21. In custody battles, you're more likely to come out on top as the court system favours your gender. If so inclined, you can also use the threat of divorce as a means of control during marriage. (You will probably also wonder why there is a marriage strike and the MGTOW movement.)
22. If you run for political office, your gender alone will be a key factor in the push for you to be elected, and there will be pressure on voters to elect you for that very reason.

Childhood, Education, and Work

23. You can pretend there is bias against you in education, even though your gender currently does better at all levels of it.
24. You can gain a degree in arts, education, or social science while knowing those degrees lead to less well-paid jobs, then complain about the wage gap. You can factor satisfaction, comfort, location, and flexible hours into your job choice and still expect to be able to buy a house. You can use the wage gap as a means to demand corporate positions, while taking no interest in gender equality in the dirty, difficult, or dangerous jobs usually done by men.
25. You can use the genuine victimisation of women in history to whom you have no connection as a means to demand special powers and opportunities for yourself on the basis of what 'we' have suffered.

That is twenty-five examples, and that is enough to at least make a dent in the idea that all life's advantages go in favour of men and against women.

That also concludes my brief look at the '160+ Examples of Male Privilege in All Areas of Life.' In my view, while some of the items are valid, others are not. If people are at all persuaded by my words, perhaps we can move on from the concept of male privilege, the misplaced envy upon which it is based, and the undue bitterness to which it leads.

Having said that, there will be plenty of feminists quite unmoved by anything I have written. They will continue to believe in male privilege, and persist in the notion that men are better off than women in almost all areas of life. There is nothing that I or anyone else could say that would ever change their minds. And to those people, I have only one word to say. It is a word that may change the world. It is a word that may save the world, or even create a new one altogether. That word is...

Fecunda.

18
A Dream of Fecunda

How long have we had feminism? It seems like eternity but it's only about fifty years since it really fired up. In those fifty years, there have been thousands of books, talks, and courses on the subject, but we're still no closer to gender Utopia. I reckon it's time to seize the moment and quit while we're behind. We must rise as one people and many genders and say *Enough*! After all this talk, after all this trash, it's time to give Fecunda a go.

And what is Fecunda? It is a magical land; a country never darkened by evil or sin. It is a holy realm without pay gaps, privilege, or rape culture. Fecunda is a land populated only by women.

Sounds pretty good, huh? But is Fecunda a real place, or one known only in legend? Well, if it ain't real, it ought to be. Women have suffered too long at the hands of men. As one feminist said, it's only down to their 'immense compassion or immense foolishness' that they continue to co-exist with men at all. Yet we can't expect women's love to be boundless. It's time for the Dear John letter; time to go our separate ways. Women deserve a homeland. They deserve Fecunda.

The idea of Fecunda came to me in a dream. It was right after I saw *Black Panther*, that documentary about the awesome country of Wakanda in Africa. Wakanda is a really cool place with advanced technology they developed on their own, far from Western civilisation. Yet as we know, Wakanda is an ethnostate, only for Africans. Because of that, Wakanda has never had the problem of racism. It stands to reason there's no racism in an ethnostate. In the same way, an all-female Fecunda will solve the problem of sexism. That means no more domestic violence, no more man-splaining or man-spreading. In fact, no more problems at all.

Sure, there's the matter of reproduction, for without children, how can Fecunda endure? Should they take a few men as breeding slaves in a sort of reverse *Handmaid's Tale*? Better not. No hint of toxic masculinity should ever taint the holy land of Fecunda. I guess the Fecundan scientists can figure out some kind of cloning system. But that is mere detail. The immediate need is to get Fecunda up and running. Men have held women back for too long. Women have earned the right to live under matriarchy, with all-female companies, universities, and families. Let them lead the way and show us how civilisation can be done.

The Case for Fecunda

Now, Fecunda is not for all women. It's for those who have made it clear they've had enough of men. In other words, feminists.

It's for Boston academic, Suzanna Danuta Walters, who wrote a famous article called 'Why Can't We Hate Men?' Some people say feminism's a hate movement. According to Walters, it has every right to be. Fecunda is also for Laurie Penny, who's fed up with women doing all the work in relationships. It's for Roxane Gay who says that in the age of Me Too, it's time for men to confess their part in creating rape culture. It's for all the authors ripping off Margaret Atwood and putting out their own versions of *The Handmaid's Tale*. Really, it's for everyone who thinks patriarchy has them in its vice-like, invisible grip. Men are the problem? Fecunda is the solution.

It's time to give Fecunda a go. Just think of all the problems getting rid of men would instantly solve. Like I said - no gender pay gap, no rape culture, no male privilege. Fecunda would have 100% female CEOs, a complete lack of sexism, and the Me

Too movement would be about as necessary as those bicycles that fish don't ride.

If you want to do the thing properly, you could even wind the clock back to Year Zero. It's a grave injustice that women in history were denied the chance to make all the great inventions and discoveries. A Stone Age Fecunda would give girls the chance to shine. Let the female Newtons and Darwins emerge as they will.

Or perhaps that is a bridge too far. Fecunda may be a social Utopia, but if it is to compete with other nations, let it have access to the knowledge male privilege has produced. Let Fecunda begin on an equal footing with everyone else. Then, it may shine as the model of what human potential can achieve once patriarchy is vanquished once and for all.

Trouble in Paradise?

In theory, Fecunda should be exactly what feminists want. Let them keep all the advantages of modern life, but remove the one blight on their lives: men and the patriarchy. They could build their own society from the ground up. What could possibly go wrong? Well, maybe a couple of things.

The first problem would be finding women to do all the hard, nasty, or dangerous jobs normally done by men. The garbage collection, building, manual labour, and so on. There'd be no more men to do all that stuff. There'd also be no more men at the top running, inventing, or achieving things from which all others benefit. Still, there's no reason women can't step up and start doing all this. That's what they want, isn't it?

The second problem would be mental. Being human and living a happy life is difficult. All this time feminists have told themselves their problems are caused by men and the patriarchy. After living in that whole Excuse Culture, what are they going to do when the Great Excuse is removed?

Having played the blame game so long, they'll find it extremely hard to change - which is one reason they'll never leave. But imagine if they did. In Fecunda, there'd be no more blaming men for everything and thanking them for nothing. No more the eternal cop out. No more thinking 'I could be anything but for the cursed patriarchy!'

When your whole mindset is one of grievance, this mode of thinking isn't easy to give up. If a whole country was formed with people who think like this, it would be only a matter of time before a new scapegoat was found. Some new form of privilege or systemic unfairness would soon be discovered.

You can see this in the recent backlash against white feminists from women of colour. It is almost a matter of *schadenfraude* to see white feminists being chastised over their privilege, power, and even - Heaven forbid - the pay gap between black and white women. Still, we'd better not have any of that mean old *schadenfraude* stuff around here. It might lead to fantasies about what happens when people who do nothing but complain are forced to live with each other.

The Skeptics' Attack on Fecunda

I'm not the first to dream of Fecunda. Of course, there were the lesbian separatists in the 1970s, but as recently as 2018 - at the height of the Brett Kavanaugh furore - some visionary on Twitter said, *Ladies, fuck it all. Let's start our own damn country!*

This set off a storm of replies. The most succinct of these was, '*And yet you're still here.*'

Some insinuated an all-female country might not be a place of peace and harmony. '*The weekly civil wars would be draining,*' said one. '*Y'all would hate each other in 4 days,*' said another. A less optimistic forecast was, '*I'd give your country about 2 hours before it burns to the ground.'* One woman tweeted, *'A country with only feminists in it? I think I've heard of that one. It's called Hell. But please go.'*

Some men were in favour of an all-female country, albeit for different reasons. *'You can take the blame for a while,'* said one guy. Another echoed the sentiment. *'Do it. There will be no way you can blame men for your problems!'* Another said, *'For the love of GOD, please do. Take all the Feminists and the Soy-boy fruitcake men. Let me know where to donate. It'll take you less than a year to have your own civil war when you realize that men AREN'T your problem, YOU are.'*

This was all terribly unfair. As one girl protested, *'It's funny how men think women can't run their own country because omg "women hate women," like they didn't create the systemic internalised misogyny to begin with.'* So it looks like in Fecunda men can still take the blame when things go wrong, even if they're not there.

Then again, some women were keen to try it. *'I'm in!'* one tweeted. *'I offer super mad admin, commercial and legal skills... as well as being a homemaker.'* Now, while it's true those skills are useful in any modern economy, several replies showed a concern that other jobs might be harder to fill:

I'm curious about this proposal. I'm interested to see if you'll find enough workforce to construct the buildings, the roads, bridges, the power plants. Then there's the sewage plants, the plumbing, the mining, et al. This would be fascinating and educational.

Go ahead. Some things to ponder. 1. What's your constitution look like? 2. Who collects the resources? How are they distributed? 3. What's your medium of exchange? 4. How do you protect yourselves? 5. Have a draft? Mandatory military service? I've got more when you're done.

Who collects the garbage? Who climbs the cell phone towers? Who pumps your oil? Who frames your houses? Who defends your freedom? Hint: It's not feminist ink spillers with ZERO job skills.

Perceptive readers will pick up a hint of skepticism at the idea that a women-only country could work. Still, pioneers have always been mocked for having the guts to try something new. They laughed at Columbus when he set off for the New World. They laughed at Julius Caesar when he tried to conquer Ancient Britain. They laughed at Jimmy Jones when he took his People's Temple to the tropical paradise of Guyana.

Don't laugh. Goddamn it, let's give Fecunda a try! Feminists have been saying for years women can do anything men can. Perhaps they're right. Yet until the experiment is tried, it's all hypothetical - and talk is cheap. That's why Fecunda is the perfect chance for women to finally achieve their full potential away from the shackles of patriarchy and the soul-crushing privilege of men. All together now - Give Fecunda a Go!

As for who would rule, there's no shortage of high profile leaders who could step up as Fecunda's first president: Angela Merkel, Julia Gillard, or Justin Trudeau, just to name a few. Hillary might even step into the breach if she's got nothing better to do. Maybe whoever it is could make some terrible empathy-based decisions like having open borders or something. Then again, that would defeat the point, wouldn't it? Fecunda is all about keeping the right ones in and the wrong ones out.

Envy 10, Empathy 0

This chapter has been facetious in tone so far, but has a more serious intent. It's a response to what seems to be a systematic resentment of men by feminists.

Contrary to feminist belief, most Western men are not princes, lords, or playboys. We do not have lives of astonishing ease, free of troubles and sorrow.

Men are getting pretty tired of the *Envy 10, Empathy 0* view of them. We're sick of being blamed for everything and thanked for nothing. We're sick of being a 'we' at all. Men are individuals, not part of a team that can be blamed for every problem, real or imagined, women think they have. We are not a gestalt entity to be blamed for the crimes of our worst members.

But if feminists really think men are the problem, Fecunda is the solution. They should leave and establish their own society. Let's see if it leads to any kind of Utopia.

Perhaps it will. Inga Muscio seems keen on the thought of an all-female space. In her magnum opus, *Cunt: A Declaration of Independence*, she describes the life changing experience of attending the Michigan Womyn's Music Festival, where it's not only the music that's female. The gatekeepers, bus drivers, and every other role is taken by women. Indeed the only men allowed to enter the site are there to empty the porta-loos.

Muscio contrasts this with regular life, where she cannot leave her home without being immersed in a male-created world. The cars, streets, and buildings are the result of men's labour and design. Even the songs on the radio, or the movies she sees advertised, have been made by men.

This is quintessential feminist discontent. Instead of seeing our civilisation as something to be proud of or grateful for, it's a source of annoyance. The whole damn thing is a tiresome imposition on women. To be fair, Muscio's point is the frustration that women haven't had more of a hand in creating it - and *Cunt* certainly *is* a good book. Yet in this section (from pages 206-07) the antagonism to men is so strong that maybe it's time to trial some kind of gender apartheid. Why not? Why *not* trial an all female country where women can run the show? It's time to replace the complaining with action. Fecunda would be like the Michigan Womyn's Festival, but all the time. The only problem is the Fecundans will have to empty their own porta-loos.

Is feminism a hate movement? The official answer is no, but it does seem to be angrier than ever the last few years. My city's main newspaper runs anti-male stories daily. One journalist used it to proclaim the Me Too movement a revolt against aeons of oppression. Another, writing after the murder of a young woman, raged against men as a class and said it was an act of folly for women to keep partnering with them at all.

In her infamous 'Why Can't We Hate Men?' essay, Suzanna Danuta Walters argues that hate is justified. She says that right around the world, women suffer at the hands of men, just as they have through history. Men are responsible for centuries of woe and the only way they can make amends is to get out of the way. She calls on men to give up all leadership positions and hand power to women to make up for all the damage they've caused.

Some expressions of hate are even more direct. During the Brett Kavanaugh affair, a lady I'll call Amelia was outraged by all the men defending Kavanaugh on social media. She tweeted that they all deserved horrible deaths and feminists would 'laugh as they take their last gasps,' before castrating their corpses and feeding them to pigs.

As an aside, Amelia recently defended free speech on Twitter. I tweeted a reply: 'For once I agree with you, Amelia.' 'You might agree with me on a few other things too,' she answered. Not sure how to take this, I tweeted, 'You may be right,' before returning to meditate on my hopes for Fecunda.

So, let's repeat: Men are the problem. Fecunda is the solution. If Danuta Walters wants women to rule, she could keep slogging away in the countries clogged up with men, but why not just move to Fecunda? Imagine how much women can achieve once their main problem is removed once and for all. I mean, on Christmas Day 2018, someone called 'Feminist Next Door' sent out a special festive tweet on the same topic. The gist of it was to imagine that men vanished from the world for 24 hours. Mind you, they would not be harmed, just absent.

The day men vanished need not be Christmas Day itself. It could be any day. But it would be just *like* Christmas for people like 'Feminist Next Door.' The idea was for women to imagine what they could do on that joyful day, and given the nobility of the sentiment, let's forgive her for ripping off Andrea Dworkin. A couple of months later, FND answered a male heckler who said something rude about International Women's Day. She said the other 364 days of the year were all International Men's Day, so the heckler should shut up and let women have their one special day.

The trouble is 'Feminist Next Door' is way too modest in her demands. 24 hours? What can you do in 24 hours? You need at least 24 *years* to see what women can really achieve. It's just possible that after 24 years, Fecunda might be the greatest country in the entire world, a superpower to rival Wakanda itself. In Fecunda, it will be International Women's Day 365 days a year.

Rape Culture and Collective Guilt

As mentioned, this chapter has been rather flippant so far, but will now turn to a serious topic - the question of whether men as a class are responsible for individual crimes against women, and whether this entitles women to hate them. It is after such crimes, at least in my country, Australia, that feminist vitriol against men reaches peak intensity.

In June, 2018, a young woman named Eurydice Dixon was raped and murdered in a Melbourne park. This awful event stirred up a lot of anger. TV host, Lisa Wilkinson, invoked *The*

Handmaid's Tale in a tearful speech. Clementine Ford wrote a scathing newspaper column lacerating men for their collective sins.

This may seem odd, given that men as a class did not murder Eurydice Dixon. In fact, she was killed by a 19 year old autistic man named Jaymes Todd. But by some interpretations of feminist theory, men as a class *did* murder Eurydice, at least indirectly. She was a victim of 'rape culture' and systemic misogyny. Thus, if men as a whole are part of creating rape culture, some feminists hold them accountable.

Soon after the murder, a police chief spoke out urging women to take precautions - being careful where they walked at night, for instance. This drew an angry response: *Why should women change their behaviour? Men are the ones who should change their behaviour. Stop raping women!*

The feminists who said this weren't just talking to rapists, but to men as a class. The idea of 'rape culture' is that we live in a misogynistic society where rape becomes normalised through various attitudes toward women and sex.

There's a well known triangular diagram used to give an overview of rape culture. It lists twenty-one types of behaviour, at four levels. On level one are rape jokes and 'locker room banter,' for instance (although a different version includes 'unequal pay' and 'sexist attitudes.') Level two has cat-calling, stalking, and 'revenge porn.' Level three includes groping and sexual coercion, while actual rape and violence are up the top on level four.

The idea is that any act, no matter how trivial, is part of a spectrum in a general climate of misogyny. This makes rape more likely to happen, or allows its perpetrators to get away with it. That means any man committing the lower level sins - even on level one - is part of creating rape culture, so is to some degree complicit in rape itself.

Strangely, plenty of non-raping men don't like this idea, and 'not-all-men-are-rapists' is a common refrain. Such protests don't impress feminist, Clementine Ford. After the Dixon murder, Ford wrote, 'I am increasingly disagreeing with the view that not all men are part of the problem, and it's because I truly think most of them don't understand that the problem is theirs to solve.'

Her column went on to harangue men over what they do to stand up for women. Do they challenge sexist comments and misogyny from their male friends? Do they stop their colleagues harassing women? She also asked if they do their share of housework and parenting, so perhaps failure to vacuum or do the dishes is part of rape culture too.

As for who is really to blame for the murder of Eurydice Dixon, the correct answer is Jaymes Todd, the young man who actually did it. But as the theory of rape culture tries to blame a whole class of people for the acts of individuals, it is worth pointing out some problems with the idea.

To do this, I'll make two analogies. The first is to do with our treatment of farm animals. If there is one class of beings with a genuine claim to being victims, it is the animals we raise and kill for food. The morality of killing animals is a separate argument that I won't go into here, but for the sake of the analogy, let's say it is wrong. If so, then all people who eat meat are complicit in this and share whatever guilt is involved.

I've recently gone towards vegetarianism, but as I still sometimes eat meat, I share in the guilt. On the other hand, you can't say vegetarians and vegans share that guilt, for the obvious reason that they don't eat meat and actively avoid doing so.

So, going back to the murder of poor Eurydice Dixon, a feminist glaring at men and snarling *you're part of the problem* is like someone scolding a group of vegans and vegetarians for their part in killing animals. Most men do not rape, and trying to smear them with some kind of collective guilt for the crimes of rogue individuals is not just unfair but absurd.

In terms of the analogy, a feminist might say being a vegan isn't enough. You have to become a PETA activist and stop people eating meat. You can't, for example, stand around at a BBQ while other people are eating sausages. You have to call them out on it or you're enabling 'carnivore culture.' But no, individuals are only responsible for their own acts. Carnivores are guilty of eating meat; vegetarians are not. Rapists are guilty of rape; non-rapists are not.

The second analogy I'll make is with Muslims as a whole being blamed for acts of terrorism. After terror acts by Muslim extremists, some people have tried to blame all Muslims, or Islam itself. It's a good parallel for feminist attempts to blame all men for individual crimes against women.

Suppose there are two types of Muslims - moderates and extremists. You can't blame the moderates for acts of terror committed by extremists. The moderates would have had no idea the atrocities were being planned, let alone executed.

You *could* argue there's a systemic hostility behind such acts. If - as some claim - the ideology of Islam is anti-Western, you could say the ideology is partly to blame for extremists' acts of terror. Yet even if that were true, you still can't blame moderate Muslims for what extremists do.

You might theorise that there's a 'terror culture' made up of anti-Western attitudes. This could be a four level spectrum like the one for rape culture. On level one are trivial acts like making anti-Western jokes or disapproving comments about Western morals. Level two might be refusing to serve Westerners in Muslim shops, or forming cultural enclaves. Actual terrorists acts would be at the top on level four. By this logic, using rape culture as a parallel, moderate Muslims who make anti-Western jokes are also guilty of acts of terror. But that is absurd.

It is true systemic hostility can lead to individual crimes as, for example, anti-Semitism in 1930s Germany led to crimes against Jews. However, there are problems with trying to push this sort of collective guilt. First, a low level offence isn't the same as one at a high level. A Muslim tut-tutting about 'Western morality' isn't as bad as one who blows up a Balinese nightclub, as happened in 2002.

Second, you could say that if 'terror culture' helps normalise acts of terror, then those who refrain from such acts are actually more moral than they would otherwise be. If terror is normal, it is *more* virtuous than usual to refrain. Likewise, if 'rape culture' normalises rape, those who live in a rape culture and *don't* rape are more moral than those who live in a non-rape culture and don't rape.

Suppose there's a culture where it's legal to take child brides, for instance. Men who *could* take child brides but don't are more moral than men who *can't* take them and don't. Obviously, cultures where child marriage is legal don't see it as immoral, but for the sake of argument let's say there are two men who believe taking child brides is morally dubious. One of them lives in Australia, the other in Pakistan. In Australia, it is illegal and socially unacceptable to take child brides. In Pakistan it is both legal and *relatively* normal. If both these men find the practice morally dubious, the man from Pakistan is the more moral for refusing to do it - because he actually *could*, but doesn't.

To go back to the animal analogy, it's both legal and acceptable to eat meat. There is no moral censure for doing it, no consequences at all. As a result, the decision to abstain, by vegans and vegetarians, is admirable because they are making a moral choice in the absence of any social pressure to do so.

Therefore, if we live in this so called 'rape culture,' where sexual assault is somehow endorsed and enabled by misogyny, men who live in it and don't rape are more moral than they would be if they *didn't* live in a rape culture.

It's a strange and fairly absurd argument to make, but that's what you get when a young woman's death is used as an excuse to shame all men for their supposed complicity.

Misogyny?

But why should we believe in rape culture in the first place? Taking the phrase literally for a moment, there's not, to my knowledge, any modern Western country where rape is permitted. Taking it more broadly, there are reasons to doubt Western culture is deeply misogynistic, as some feminists believe.

First, there's been a big push in recent times to promote women's interests, in a number of ways. Why would that happen if society was misogynistic? Feminists may reply that this is all the result of their fight for justice, but if society really was misogynistic, those reforms wouldn't get through at all.

At the same time, there's been a lot of recent anti-male sentiment. Never mind men being the butt of jokes in sitcoms, or the steady stream of anti-male ad campaigns. You actually have in our universities the systematic denigration of men, and especially white men, as being somehow to blame for all the world's problems. Society is misogynistic? If anything, it's increasingly misandric.

Just look at the main newspaper in my city. On any given day, you'll find several pro-female and anti-male articles. It's surely only a matter of time before the *Sydney Morning Herald* renames itself the *Sydney Morning Feminist.*

If we believe some theorists, the murder of Eurydice Dixon is the end result of systemic misogyny. 'Rape culture' is a spectrum of inter-connected behaviour, and any man who engages in a sexist act at the low level is also contributing to rape. So if we could just reform men and get rid of rape culture as a whole, acts of rape and murder will also cease.

Call me a skeptic, but if you really think calling out sexist jokes at the office Christmas party is going to stop some psychopath murdering a random woman in a city park, well, good luck with that.

Do rapist-murderers do it because they hate women? No doubt some do, but others won't have thought it through that far. Obviously, some are immoral, acting from pure malice. Others are amoral in that they don't care about the ethics of their actions, or the effect on others. They're indifferent to moral questions. A third type are probably just stupid, with poor impulse control and no understanding of consequences. A fourth type are mentally ill and disturbed. The idea that all these men commit their crimes due to society-wide misogyny seems like a one-size-fits-all theory.

There's a more basic reason why the risk of rape will never be eliminated by mere 'education.' To put it in coldly clinical terms, rape may be a side effect of a system where supply and demand are heavily out of balance. That is, when it comes to sex, one gender can get it when they don't want it and the other can't get it when they do. Under those conditions, rape will sometimes occur from a minority of men who are evil, ill, or have poor impulse control. Of course, this is not the fault of women, and none of that is any justification for rape. But it seems a simpler, more likely reason for rape than the catch all theory of 'misogyny.'

Those who think rape culture is the problem think stopping misogyny is the solution. This seems over idealistic. If you really want to address the threat of rape, better to acknowledge that, in those coldly clinical terms, sexual supply and demand are way out of balance. As a result, there will always be a small minority of ill or evil men who are a threat to women. That's the reality of it. What you can do about it is a separate question.

There's a great YouTube talk by a feminist and rape survivor, Wendy McElroy, on the fallacy of rape culture. She makes the point that if people are serious about stopping rape, it can only happen by addressing its real causes. Pushing an ideology about 'respecting women' is a different issue, worthy in its own right, but may not have much to do with stopping rape, at least in the Western world.

McElroy agrees there *are* rape cultures in some parts of the world. Cultures which permit, for example, child brides, honour killings, rape within marriage, mistreatment of low caste women, and so on. You could make a case that those sort of rape cultures *are* tied up in misogynistic views of women in general. In comparison, claims about rape culture in the West look trivial. They insult not just Western men, but those women around the world who have a genuine claim to be living in a rape culture.

Let's Make Murder Illegal

Some feminists have said it is the responsibility of men as a class to stop rape and murder. It is 'their problem to solve.' How could men actually do this? Here's a thought to get the ball rolling - why not make murder illegal?

After the Eurydice Dixon murder, men did try one thing. The Australian Senate proposed that women carry tasers, pepper spray and mace to defend themselves. That sounds like a good, proactive strategy, but it was rejected. A leading feminist was part of a senate majority who opposed the motion. They had a better idea: teach men not to assault women.

It's hard to believe an immediate, practical step was turned down on the basis of ideology - an ideology that believes stopping rape culture will stop rape. Even if you accept that premise, it would still take decades to achieve. In the meantime, why not carry some pepper spray?

Some women are angry at being asked to take precautions, but *any* person should take steps to reduce risk. Compared to women, men are far more at risk of violence in public places, so they try not to put themselves in danger. They know, for example, not to go out in King's Cross after 1am. In the days of football hooliganism in England, peaceful football fans knew to stay away from rival fan areas. Generally, there are certain bars, streets, or events you should avoid. The reality is some men *are* violent, and other men have to take whatever steps are needed: learn self defence, don't hang out with thugs, avoid bad locations after midnight. This is all routine and commonsense advice.

As for sexual assault, men don't face the same risks as women, but in the Me Too era some of them have adopted 'Mike Pence Rules.' US vice president Pence has a rule to never be alone in a room with any woman other than his wife. This is to lower the risk of a false sexual harassment allegation. High profile men would prefer the risk didn't exist, but it does - so they take precautions.

In a YouTube talk called 'Are Men Responsible for Ending Sexual Violence?' Janice Fiamengo refutes the idea that men could do so even if they tried. She says the demand that men eliminate rape conflates the truth that men have the individual power and responsibility not to commit sexual assault with the false claim they can stop it in others. It's a 'sleight of hand' indeed.

Fiamengo makes an analogy with parenting. There are some

terrible parents out there (a small minority) but it would be unfair to make parents-as-a-class bear responsibility for what the bad ones do, and useless to imply they have any power to stop it.

A Hidden Source of Misogyny

Remember that 'rape culture' is a set of misogynistic attitudes that makes offences against women more likely to occur. Let's look at this idea from another angle.

To be fair, fostering an attitude of hate towards a class of people *does* have an effect - or rather, a number of effects. One is that you feel less sympathy for that group and their problems. Another is you may feel resentment towards them, even an element of ill will. A third is you might want to have nothing to do with them. This is true of various types of people that are antagonistic to other types.

But if it's true a systematic dislike of one group for another has consequences, one might argue feminists are responsible for creating hostility not just towards men as a class, but towards women as a class. How so?

Not all feminists hate men, but enough do to have real world effects. The Me Too movement, for instance, began as a protest against sleazy Hollywood moguls then turned into a much wider campaign with the potential for abuse. As Fiamengo said, 'all women have now acquired a deadly weapon...and a significant minority are willing or even eager to use it.'

No doubt *some* feminists are delighted to bring down as many powerful men as possible. Some of those men deserve it, others do not. Yet if some innocent men go down as collateral damage, these feminists will shrug their shoulders, talk about male tears, and see it as some kind of payback.

It's one thing to incite resentment of men, but a side effect is that you also incite resentment of women. It may seem to feminists that their efforts to help women can do nothing but good. Where their causes are just, they may be right.

They may also think they're helping women when they lie about the gender pay gap, give a one-sided view of domestic violence, or support a pro-female / anti-male agenda in the media and education. In the short term, these actions may help women, up to a point. What they also do is create a strong tide of resentment against women as a class.

Among the many fruits of this are the MGTOW movement, the refusal of some male bosses to mentor women in the wake of Me Too, less sympathy for women, strong antipathy to feminism as a cause, and less inclination to support pro-women reforms one might otherwise agree with.

Apparently, rape culture is made of misogyny. But if misogyny means antagonism towards women, it's possible third-wave feminism has created more antagonism than anyone else ever could. Feminism at its worst is self-defeating because it doesn't inspire either respect or support for its causes - and feminism is at its worst all too often these days.

The movement may have begun as a just cause, but over the years it has evolved into a hate movement. Why can't we hate men? says Suzanna Danuta Walters. Well, sure, you can. Just do it somewhere else.

In Fecunda.

What is feminism today? Rape culture. Me Too. The gender pay gap. Envy 10, Empathy 0. Men-bad-women-good. Blaming men for everything and thanking them for nothing. And let's not forget that men as a class are supposedly complicit in the rape and murder of Eurydice Dixon. In reality, such an event could only appal any moral man.

Soon after Eurydice Dixon's death, Clementine Ford wrote an angry newspaper column berating men. As it was written in the emotional aftermath of the murder, one might forgive some over-statement. Yet the passage below is from her book, published months later, with only minor changes from the original column.

> It is a mark of either immense compassion or immense foolishness that women continue to throw ourselves into the act of loving men despite amassing a lifetime of experiences that tell us how dangerous this decision can be. I am increasingly disagreeing with the view that not all men are part of the problem, and it's because I truly think most of them don't understand that the problem is theirs to solve...
>
> Women don't need to be told to look for the goodness in men, because we try our damnedest to find it every day. We work hard to nurture it, even as we're told to be grateful for it. For our own survival, women must believe that not all men are the enemy.

I've read both of Ford's books and many of her columns and was surprised by her claims about looking for men's goodness. Perhaps in her personal life she tries her damnedest to find the goodness in men, but she sure doesn't in her published work. On the contrary, she seems to try her damnedest to find the worst in them.

Clementine Ford is entitled to her views. She's even entitled to broadcast them through books and newspaper columns. But if she really thinks women take their lives in their hands by partnering with men, perhaps it's time to go our separate ways.

It's time to give feminists the space and opportunity they need. Go, and may the Goddess go with you. Goodbye Suzanna. Goodbye Amelia. Goodbye to all the feminists convinced they live in *The Handmaid's Tale*. Please go - with our blessings and good wishes. We wish you well in establishing the Republic of Fecunda and creating your dream country free from our eternal sabotage. Go in peace - and good luck.

19

The Surprising Liberation

Some people speak of structures of oppression. There are also structures of belief. The conceptual house of feminism is held up by five main pillars: ideas about patriarchy, sexism, male privilege, sexual assault, and the gender pay gap.

While the risk of sexual assault is real and there's still some sexism, the other pillars are largely illusions. The gender pay gap isn't a crime against women. Neither are Western women controlled by a powerful force called the patriarchy. As for the fifth pillar - male privilege - that is the central false idea holding up the entire structure.

As mentioned, a recent debate asked the question 'Is male privilege bullshit?' So, is it? On the whole, yes. The theory of male privilege says that nearly all life's advantages go in favour of men. Most of this book has been about refuting the idea. Of course, for some people, no argument could ever change their mind. But why? That brings us to the final problem in my list of twenty-five.

Problem 25 - Addicted to Feminism

Many feminists will believe in male privilege despite all arguments against it. Strangely, even if they are wrong, that doesn't mean they're lying. Sure, some are liars, but others are seeing the world as it appears through the lens of feminist ideology. They truly see and experience a world which seems to justify their beliefs. It isn't lying, so much as being under the spell of a belief system that becomes almost hypnotic. The evidence seems to be everywhere. They fall victim to 'confirmation bias' - 'the tendency to search for, interpret, favour, and recall information in a way that confirms one's pre-existing beliefs.'

Everyone does this to some degree, and feminists more than most. They are deeply committed to the idea that everything goes against women. Why are they so determined to believe this? Let's return to the incident of *The Red Pill* film and the protests against it.

In *The Red Pill*, Cassie Jaye spoke to men's rights activists. She was a feminist when she began making the film but gradually changed her mind. She came to realise not everything was in favour of men after all.

In an odd way, Jaye's film could have been good news for feminists. Maybe women aren't so badly off. But deep at the heart of feminism is the idea of women as a maligned underclass, forever getting the short end of the stick. Challenges to this idea aren't good news, they're deeply alarming!

In chapter two, I wrote:

> One problem with the idea of male-privilege-as-fact is that the group who hates it the most - feminists - also owe their existence to it. What happens if male privilege comes to an end? Does that also mean the end of feminism?

> It's an odd dynamic. A group has a strong opposition to something but also a vested interest in believing it, as it is their *raison d'être* and the motor that drives them forward. Though they may hate it, feminists have stronger motivation to believe in male privilege than to disbelieve it. This can lead to a questionable relationship with the evidence.

In short, feminists are deeply committed to the idea of male privilege whether it's true or not. By rejecting the idea, Cassie Jaye became a heretic. A feminist apostate. These religious terms are fitting, because feminism today is indeed a sort of cult. A secular, state-sponsored cult, but a cult nonetheless. It is a fanatical movement with a strong us vs them mentality, a will to power, and a world-changing mission they see as a holy crusade.

This is a cult with many members, most of whom have no wish to leave. They are addicted to feminism. Though Western women are no longer enslaved they will fight to the death for the idea that they are, and scorn bitterly the bearer of any good news to the contrary.

The Surprising Liberation

At this point, you might ask if it's really all worth it. Why carry a sense of grievance if you don't have to? The surprising liberation for some feminists might be the following simple step: stop believing in male privilege.

It's a bizarre concept, I know, but imagine the weight off the shoulders of laying this burden down. The astounding revelation should be that most men are not particularly better off, luckier, or more blessed than most women. In the same way, most women are not particularly worse off, unluckier, or more cursed than most men. This is in the Western world, of course. Outside is another story, but the time is long overdue to drop the idea that Western women are oppressed.

Women have nothing to lose but their chains, especially the ones that don't really exist.

Why Oppose Feminism?

Some feminists don't understand why their cause attracts such hostility. They still think their fight is for justice and equality. If so, anti-feminists can only be seen as having evil motives. They must be jealous, or spiteful, or want to keep women down. They can only be driven by hate.

Well, it is not so much that people hate feminism. They simply despise it. For while feminism may have begun as a liberation movement, it is now something else. There were scenes filmed at a Canadian University where male students were forced to stand in front of a class and confess their male privilege. It looks like something out of a socialist re-education purge. This is just one example of a cultish movement that thinks the role of universities is to recruit foot soldiers for the Glorious Revolution.

People who *actually* believe in justice and equality see little of it in today's feminism. They despise it because it is a mockery of those ideals. In fact, when it comes to why people dislike feminism, there are so many reasons, so little time. So what are the *main* reasons?

Could it be feminists' need to divide people into teams, then demand special treatment for their own? Perhaps it's the attempt by today's women to use historic injustices they never suffered to gain advantages from those who never committed them. Or is it the relentless self bias in their perception of each and every issue?

Is it feminists' need to control the debate on gender issues, and their thuggish attempts to silence anyone else? Perhaps it is the droning whine, melodious as a leaf blower, that powers their mission to complain their way to the top. Is it the hypocrisy of wanting equality but also special treatment?

Or is it something more basic - that feminism, as it is today, doesn't encourage women to be at their best, but at their worst? It was supposed to produce a generation of tough, competent, and admirable girls. While feminism may produce some strong women, it also creates a lot of terrible ones. For some detail on this, a YouTube video by Janice Fiamengo called 'Feminism as a Victim Mentality Disorder' is right on point.

Fiamengo is an ex-feminist who became an outspoken critic. As a fulltime academic in a Canadian university, she spent many years in a feminist environment. Some of her reasons for opposing it are given in a video talk called 'Female White Knights.' By any measure, Fiamengo appears to be a reasonable person, and although the following is strongly worded it is delivered in her usual calm manner.

> I don't want to live any longer in a culture in which I and most people submit to lies about women's victimization and male privilege. It feels crazy and sick. I particularly don't want to live in a society in which every time I open a newspaper I have to suppress a roar of disgust because there's yet another womanly demand for special privileges or government sponsored perks, or more complaints, jealousies and resentment directed at men...

> You see I'm at the point where I can hardly bear to read newspapers without fear of apoplectic fits. I definitely don't want to spend the next twenty or thirty years or however much longer I have left on this Earth in a society that gives women permission, really encourages women, almost mandates them to be at their worst - selfish, hypocritical, superficial, amoral, mean spirited, manipulative and vindictive. It's not good for my self-respect as a woman.

> I don't want to live in a culture that turns women into raging children supposedly too scared to attend an astronomy conference or even walk down the street for fear of sexual harassment, but *not* too scared to lecture men on their evil, berate them, slander them, belittle them and call for yet more laws and

policies to make their lives more difficult in addition to the discrimination they already face in hiring, employment, family court, health care, reproductive rights, educational opportunities, government services, military conscription, etc.

I fear it's all turning me into a raving misogynist and that can't be good for my mental health. I don't want to spend the remainder of my teaching career watching the girls in my classes become ever more inclined to blame every personal failure or ordinary life setback or challenge on 'institutionalised sexism' while the boys become ever quieter, more apathetic, more unsure of themselves, more awkward, apologetic, ashamed, sad, angry, and adrift. It's painful and infuriating to witness and I suspect that one day soon I might go ballistic and launch into a gynophobic tirade in my class that will lead to my being forced to take a series of sensitivity workshops and issue a public apology...

Furthermore, it's definitely in my self interest to live in a sane world. A world in which the most talented, capable, and hard working people - often men as it turns out - are in charge. A world that holds me and other women to a standard of achievement rather than giving us top jobs and special perks just because we're women. I want all the perks done away with for good because they're a moral hazard to me and to all women.

Most fundamentally, I don't want to live in a world that makes me so disgusted and repulsed by the behaviour of my own sex that it forces me to wonder whether *I'm* really a selfish narcissistic monster too. There sure do seem to be a lot of nasty narcissists out there, enabled by a society gone mad over poor-woman-hysteria.

When I read that a recent American survey found that 44% of college women don't believe a nod of agreement is sufficient to count as sexual consent, in other words that a woman who nodded to the boy she's making out with can later claim she was raped.

When I read about cases such as that involving (a young woman) who lied about her father sexually abusing her to punish him and only admitted her lie after her father spent nine years in jail and nothing is going to happen to her because - you guessed it - if she were punished it might prevent *other* liars from coming forward to put their innocent fathers in jail.

When I read about (a married woman) getting off with a probationary sentence for paying a man to kill her husband, and who still retains custody of their child. When I see a statement by (a female Australian CEO) ...stating with relish that well qualified men will simply have to lose their jobs to make it possible for all government boards to have fifty percent female representation, when she has the nerve to say of the men they're not going to want to lose their jobs but that's just the way it is.

When I read this and so much more, I am sickened and humiliated and almost totally turned off by the female half of humanity. Thank God for (anti-feminists) Karen and Daphne and Janet and others. Ultimately I just don't want the horror of seeing men crippled in the way feminism has crippled them. I can't be who I want to be in the world if that's being done to men.

To clarify one point against those who would quote it out of context, Fiamengo says the 'most talented, capable, and hard working people' should be in charge. That doesn't mean it should be men. If those people are women, Fiamengo would fully endorse them. What she objects to are the perks and privileges of affirmative action. Fiamengo wants to take gender out of the equation. The best people should be appointed, whatever their sex.

Fiamengo is strongly spoken because she has seen third-wave feminism up close, and seen it for what it is - as a sort of state-sanctioned mass cult that has inflicted a good deal of damage. It's part of a wider insanity, which is identity politics and the Glorious Revolution.

So, how's that revolution going so far? Take a look around you. The Glorious Revolution isn't a hypothetical - it's happening now. Look at the world today and see what the revolution has created. Whole sections of the population hate and despise each other. While, in a way, it's fascinating to see such a fractured and insane world, in practical terms the whole thing is a shambles. As for feminism's part in that, there's now probably more hatred between men and women than ever before. Good job.

Likely Responses to This Book

If this book ever reaches the attention of actual feminists, one might anticipate four main types of response.

The first will be to just write it off as misogyny and ignore it. A weak response, but fairly predictable.

The second will be to try to 'destroy' the book, one way or

another. Slander it, lie about it, perhaps try to ban it altogether. Again, a weak response, and again quite likely - and it would only prove my point.

The third would be to prove me wrong and refute my arguments. That would be a fair response, and if feminists can do it successfully, good for them.

The fourth response would be to realise that many of the recent critics of feminism have a point. Honourable feminists might realise their movement has some flaws that need fixing. Instead of taking criticism as a mortal offence, the best response would be some detailed self reflection.

Although a brutal self examination is overdue, it probably won't happen. For a movement certain it owns the high moral ground, it won't be easy to admit parts of it are ethically rotten. Many feminists will find it impossible to even consider the idea. Fine, they can carry on as they are - but feminism will continue to be widely despised. Feminists should realise they haven't owned the high moral ground for a long, long time. They're not even paying rent, just squatting, and hurling insults at anyone passing by.

Feminism began with good ideals, and there are surely plenty of good people working within it. If so, it's time for the honourable feminists to make major reforms. They should call their own movement to account. There should be a major self examination, a pruning of the dead wood, and a purge of the corruption and silly ideas that have crept in.

Some have already been doing that, such as the brilliant Camille Paglia, which is one reason plenty of feminists hate her. If only there were more like Paglia.

Feminism should stage a new revolt - not against patriarchy, but against itself. Feminists should rip off the self-bias blinders, get out of their echo chamber, and fix what's gone wrong. They should make a big bonfire and toss in all the ideological dead wood. The poor-me victim mentality should be first onto the flames, then the whole Excuse Culture rort. Toss in the men-bad-women-good premise, along with the bogus stats on domestic violence and campus sexual assault. Then the misandry, the bias, and the self righteous zeal. All of it, into the flames.

Then when the purge is complete, feminism could emerge as a stronger movement, one worthy of respect. It will be a movement that no longer makes cowardly attempts to silence its critics. It will be one that holds women to account rather than endlessly excusing them. One that looks beyond its own myopic ideas of justice and sees a broader version of that concept. It will be a movement that scorns lies, bullying, and hypocrisy rather than enabling them.

Exiting the Cult

Of course, none of this will ever happen. There'll be no self criticism, no internal review. That's not what fanatics do. If feminists' real motivation is power, questions of ethics and truth would only get in the way.

Feminism does not exist alone, but as part of the wider political left, fighting for its Glorious Revolution. Despite the shambles it has created so far, the revolution was based on good intentions. Leftists really do believe in a world of equality where all races and genders share in the power, wealth, and other manifestations of worldly success. No matter how good the intentions, it all looks terribly cult-like today.

If nothing more, at least we can hope there are a few individuals prepared to leave the cult behind. There may be college students who can see past their gender studies indoctrination, or some honourable feminists who see that the cause they once loved is no longer worthy.

If they do walk away, let them come in peace. There should be no recriminations, no snide remarks. There's no shame in making mistakes, but there is honour in admitting to them. Doing this takes self awareness, a sense of the bigger picture, and the realisation that you might be wrong. Feminists rarely admit mistakes, not because they are never wrong, but because their need to occupy the high moral ground is so intense.

Perhaps eventually we'll go past today's insanity and enter a new phase. The philosopher, Johann Fichte, had a theory that history moves through stages he called thesis, antithesis, and synthesis. That means the world is a certain way, then there's a strong over-reaction as it goes the other way, and finally a compromise between the two extremes. Or in other words - boy meets girl, boy loses girl, boy and girl get back together.

In terms of the gender war, that could loosely translate like this. First there was what feminists see as a male-dominated patriarchal world. The feminist revolution was the reaction against that. Eventually, we may reach a third stage which is a compromise.

If we could keep the best reforms of feminism but jettison the mistakes, perhaps we can reach a stage where the two genders no longer hate each other and we regain some kind of unity.

Ten Solutions

This book is based on the idea of twenty-five *problems*. Here are some solutions which might help.

I - Admit it if Things Are Unfair

Many of second-wave feminism's causes were fair and led to reasonable reforms. If there are still injustices today, we should fix them - but they must be real injustices, not pretend ones.

In the same way, if there is still actual sexism and misogyny today, it should be opposed. Dropping any spurious claims of sexism and misogyny would help in getting rid of the real stuff.

II - Aim for Real Equality

Equality of opportunity is good, equality of outcome is not. We should stop confusing the two.

Let's admit that both men and women are capable of good and evil, and so adopt a realistic view of human nature.

In dealing with people professionally, we can start with the assumption both genders are equally capable and go from there. From that point, judge individuals on merit by their actions.

Women will never have real equality until they stop demanding special favours. Those who want real equality won't ask for favours and will win everyone's respect.

III - Move on From the Gender Fixation

There's a famous line that says feminism is based on the radical idea that women are people.

But by the way, did you hear about that female astronaut? The remarkable chess champion who was a woman? Did you know women do better in school but earn less? I heard the number of women in STEM has gone up by 1.5%. Do you like women's sports? Hillary is a woman. Oh, and by the way, did you hear about that woman?

We will never have gender equality until we move on from the obsession with gender. Guess what? Someone who did something is a male or a female. How interesting.

(Note - the famous line is paraphrased from a great quote by feminist, Marie Shear.)

IV - Stop Blaming Others For What They Can't Control, What You Can Control, and What Nobody Can Control

Men should get together as a group and have a meeting about stopping rape. No, that's impossible. Social Expectations make all our main life decisions for us. No they don't. Women age faster and it's not fair. Take it up with God, evolution, or whoever else you see as responsible, because it's nothing to do with men.

V - Discriminate

We discriminate when we fail to discriminate.

There are a lot of white males. There are many Asian females. There are plenty of people of colour. Some people are gay. Others are straight. There are also Muslims, Christians, and atheists. And a thousand other categories.

While such groups have things in common, they are made up of individuals. Treat them as such, not as part of a collective. Discriminate.

Identity politics is one of the most divisive ideologies ever contrived. Instead of treating it with reverence or fear, as is common today, greet it with a laugh or a yawn. Identity politics originally had a point, but has flogged itself into oblivion through over-use. Using victimhood as a tool of empowerment is a bad mental habit, and a rort that has to end.

VI - Reform Universities

Universities are supposed to teach students how to think, not what to think. They're not meant to be recruitment centres for the Glorious Revolution.

If universities are now staffed by ideologues rather than intellectuals, and feature group-think not free-think, it's time to revolt against the revolutionaries. This is not how universities are supposed to work. In their present form, they are an embarrassment to our civilisation and to themselves.

VII - Be Honest and Self Aware

It's time to stop pretending we're still living in 1970, that all domestic violence goes one way, or that there's no female privilege.

If we are biased towards our own causes, at least admit it and realise it can affect our perception of any given situation.

VIII - Allow Criticism

If your group doesn't allow criticism, you're a cult.

IX - Gratitude as a Novel Concept

Ever had a friend who is always complaining? Third-wave feminism is that friend. Never happy, always whining. Don't hang out with that friend. Don't *be* that friend.

It's said that one of the key causes of happiness is having a sense of gratitude. Imagine that. Being grateful for what you have. It's a radical concept and worth a try!

X - Let's End the Gender War

The gender war will end when feminists give up the idea that women are engaged in some kind of class warfare with men, and when they stop believing in the false concept of male privilege. This will allow them to move away from the current Envy 10 Empathy 0 state of mind, and drag it back to at least Envy 5 Empathy 5.

From there, anything is possible.

Notes

Chapter 3

Harris, S. 'Now saying genius or brilliant can alienate female students.' *Daily Mail*, 13th June, 2017.

Chapter 4

The Karen Straughan quote featured in Cassie Jaye's film, *The Red Pill*.

The Milo quote is from a YouTube video, but I've lost track of which one. Ditto for the Cassie Jaye video comments, and the Swedish feminist in chapter 5. Anyone who has them, feel free to send to the publisher.

Hamad, R. 'There is no 'debate' to be had over the existence of male privilege.' *Sydney Morning Herald*, 31st May, 2017.

Chapter 5

Bawer, B. *The Victims' Revolution*. Broadside Books, USA. 2012.

Elam, P, Fiamengo, J, Golden, T. *Regarding Men*, Episode 20: 'Happy Father's Day, You Piece of Shit.' YouTube. 2019.

Chapter 6-7

All Clementine Ford quotes are from chapters 4-8 of *Boys Will Be Boys*, Allen & Unwin. Australia. 2018.

Chapter 7

Elam, P. 'How to Get Your Man to Punch You in the Face.' YouTube. 2018.

Elam, P. 'Violent Men: When Harry Met Mary,' YouTube. 2017.

Chapter 10

Chakrabarti, S. *Of Women in the 21st Century*. Penguin, UK. 2018.

Asher, R. *Shattered: Modern Motherhood and the Illusion of Equality*. Vintage. UK. 2012.

Nemko, M. 'Men as Beasts of Burden.' *A Voice for Men*. March 18, 2018.

Nemko, M. 'The Real Reason so few Women are in the Boardroom.' *A Voice for Men*, March 28, 2018.

Chapter 11

Straughan, K. 'The Tyranny of Female Hypoagency.' YouTube. 2012.

Irvine, J. 'Acting Wife?' How men can really help women in the workforce.' *Sydney Morning Herald*, February 25, 2018.

Nemko, M. 'The Real Reason so few Women are in the Boardroom.' *A Voice for Men*, March 28, 2018.

Chapter 12

Goad, J. 'Smashing Through the Glass Coffin.' *Taki's Mag*. January, 2016.

Farrell, W. *The Myth of Male Power*. Simon & Schuster, USA, 1993.

Straughan, K. Channel 4, 'Jordan Peterson Interview: My Thoughts.' YouTube. 2018.

Chapter 13

Johnson, M. '160+ Examples of Male Privilege in all Areas of Life.' *Everyday Feminism*. 2016.

Chapter 15

Hoff Summers, C. *The War Against Boys*. Simon & Schuster, USA. 2000.

Chapter 16

Harinam, V & Henderson, R. 'Political Moderates Are Lying.' *Quillette*. July 2, 2018.

Chapter 18

Muscio: *Cunt, A Declaration of Independence*. Seal Press. USA 2002.

McElroy, W. 'Fallacy of the Rape Culture.' YouTube. 2014.

Ford, C. *Boys Will Be Boys*. Allen & Unwin, Australia, 2018

Fiamengo, J. 'Are Men Responsible for Ending Sexual Violence?' Fiamengo Files, Episode 72. YouTube, 2017.

Chapter 19

Fiamengo, J. 'Feminism: A Victim Mentality Disorder.' Fiamengo Files, Episode 29. YouTube, 2016.

Fiamengo, J. 'Female White Knights.' Fiamengo Files, Episode 21. YouTube, 2016.

Shear, M. *New Directions For Women*, May / June, 1986.

The confirmation bias definition is from Wikipedia.

Selected References

Asher, R. *Shattered: Modern Motherhood and the Illusion of Equality*. 2012. Vintage. UK. 2012.

Bates, L. *Misogynation*. Simon & Schuster, UK. 2018.

Benatar, D. *The Second Sexism*. Wiley-Blackwell. UK. 2012.

Crispin, J. *Why I am not a Feminist*. Black Inc, Australia. 2017.

Chakrabarti, S. *Of Women in the 21ˢᵗ Century*. Penguin, UK. 2018.

Chemaly, S. *Rage Becomes Her*. Simon & Schuster, UK. 2018.

Elam, P. *An Ear For Men*, YouTube Channel. Various Talks.

Farrell, W. *The Myth of Male Power*. Simon & Schuster, USA, 1993.

Fiamengo, J. *The Fiamengo Files*. YouTube Channel. Various Talks.

Ford, C. *Fight Like a Girl*, Allen & Unwin, Australia, 2016.

Ford, C. *Boys Will Be Boys*, Allen & Unwin, Australia, 2018.

Fox, C. *Stop Fixing Women*. UNSW Press, Australia, 2017.

Hoff Sommers, C. *The War Against Boys*. Simon & Schuster, USA. 2000.

Holdsworth, A. *Out of the Doll's House*. BBC Books, UK, 1988.

Mayer, C. *Attack of the 50 Foot Women*, HQ, Harper Collins, UK. 2018.

Moran, C. *How to be a Woman*, Harper Collins, USA, 2011.

Muscio, I. *Cunt: A Declaration of Independence*. Seal Press. USA 2002.

Paglia, C. *Free Women, Free Men*. Canongate, UK. 2018.

Sargon of Akkad. 'Why Do People Hate Feminism?' Parts 1-12. YouTube, 2015.

Straughan, K, aka Girl Writes What. YouTube Channel. Various Talks.

Also Available

Books By Duncan Smith

The Vortex Winder
The Maelstrom Ascendant
Cultown
The Tightarse Tuesday Book Club

Albums By Lighthouse XIII

Waves Upon Waves
Vortex Winder
The Maelstrom Ascendant
Cultown

Contact

Books and albums can be ordered from www.vortexwinder.com, or on Amazon or Book Depository.

Alfadex Books can be contacted on matthew.alfadex@gmail.com.

Also Available by this Author

Books

The Vortex Winder

When fading rocker, Jimmy Brandt, saves the life of an insect, his own life is forever changed. The insect turns out to be an advanced being who gives him the 'Vortex Winder,' a device which grants him a different special power each week. Each power leads to unexpected results.

Jimmy makes a comeback to rock music and records his album. Yet his comeback is a quest within a quest. Driven by the Vortex Winder, Jimmy makes an amazing journey. From a simple job interview, to a love affair in Germany, or a harrowing stint in a foreign prison, the adventures of Jimmy Brandt are always a surprise. Trailed by his mentor, Iolango, and his tormentor, Elijinx, Jimmy follows the events of his life to a stunning conclusion.

The Maelstrom Ascendant

Rocker Jimmy Brandt has given up on his dreams. He's settled down in the suburbs with his girlfriend and cat...until strange forces tempt him back to his former life. Soon he faces a choice between good and evil - and life is so rewarding when you turn to the dark side.

Flying high again, Jimmy battles divas, despots, and most of all, himself. Yet the higher you fly, the further you can fall. Only an old, forgotten friend can save him. But does he want to be saved?

Cultown

Thomas Swan forms the Milinish, a cult with an odd mix of scientific and religious beliefs.

From humble beginnings in Sydney, the Milinish moves overseas to become the fastest growing cult in America. Yet Swan's mad reign spirals out of control. Finally, on the brink of disaster, he tells all.

Here, in the ultimate inside story, Thomas Swan reveals the secrets and scandals inside the Milinish, the greatest cult of the 21st century.

> *'Exposes not just the cultishness of religion, but of science too. This is the best novel yet written on the trouble between science and religion.'*
> J. Williams, Fuse.

The Tightarse Tuesday Book Club

This new set of stories has some of Duncan Smith's best work. 'Hook Up Hell' is a comical Tinder farce, 'Badminton Boy' a superhero send-up, and 'Ghost Squad' a wry look at celebrities who pretend to write books. But it is the novella, *Marla Okadigbo*, that has caused all the fuss for its take on the hot topic of racism in modern America.

This is the story of a literary scam that takes America by storm. White male author, Winkler Jones, pens an online review of *The Handmaid's Tale*, Margaret Atwood's book about a world where women have no rights and exist only to serve men. Jones calls it 'oppression porn for feminists' and says it's only a matter of time before a black American writes a novel where slavery is restored.

Jones' crooked agent tells him to delete the review and write the slavery book himself. Jones does so, putting it out under the pen name, 'Marla Okadigbo,' supposedly a black American woman. The book is a hit until the author's true identity is revealed. It then becomes a scandal, and perception of the book changes from a story of the struggle for black liberation to one of oppression by white supremacists.

Meanwhile, Jones is haunted by the spirit of the real Marla, a black slave from the early 1800s, and feuds with his girlfriend, Sonia, a white English teacher struggling to help school students in the poor neighbourhood where she works.

Lighthouse XIII Music Albums

Waves Upon Waves
Mountain Gods, SMS: Save My Sanity, Between the Stairway and the Highway, Reaper Bones, Leuchtturm, LHXIII, Temporary Kingdom, Retro Stereo, Waves Upon Waves, New World Alchemy.

Vortex Winder
Vortex Winder, Road Rage, Trade Winds, Black Art, Life Line, Spark, Z Club, Epitaph, Elijinx, Oceanus.

The Maelstrom Ascendant
Black Phoenix, High and Mighty, The Price of Dominion, Moonlight Tiger, I for an Eye, Haunted, Death Bed Regrets, Extinction.Net, Quitter, The Maelstrom Ascendant, The Ephemeral and the Eternal.

Cultown
Amnesia, Skeptic Eclectic, Evil But Not Vile, In Nihilum, Cultown, Helix Eternal, Doom Pipers, Fallen to a Higher Place, The Scythe and the Scalpel, Triangle of Fire, Transcendence, The Cultimate Culminates.

9780987222848